This Coloring Book
Belongs To

_____

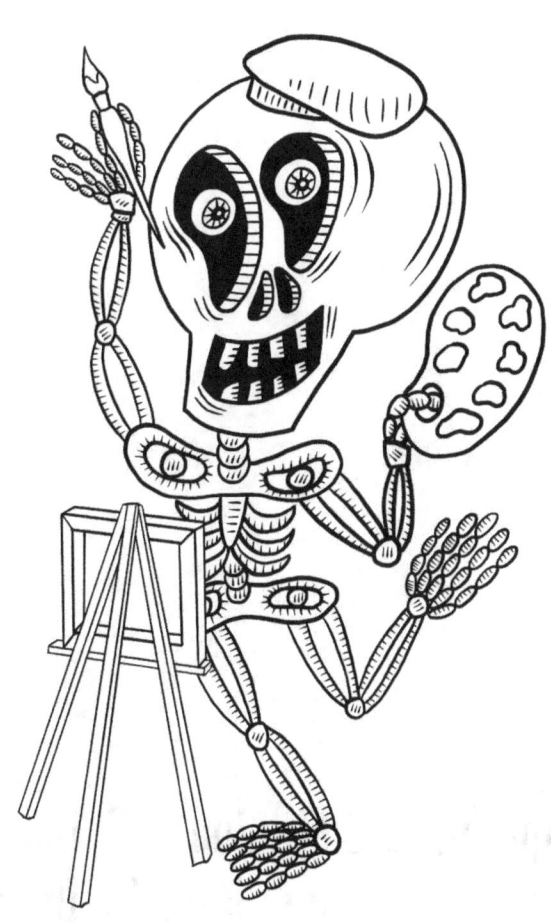

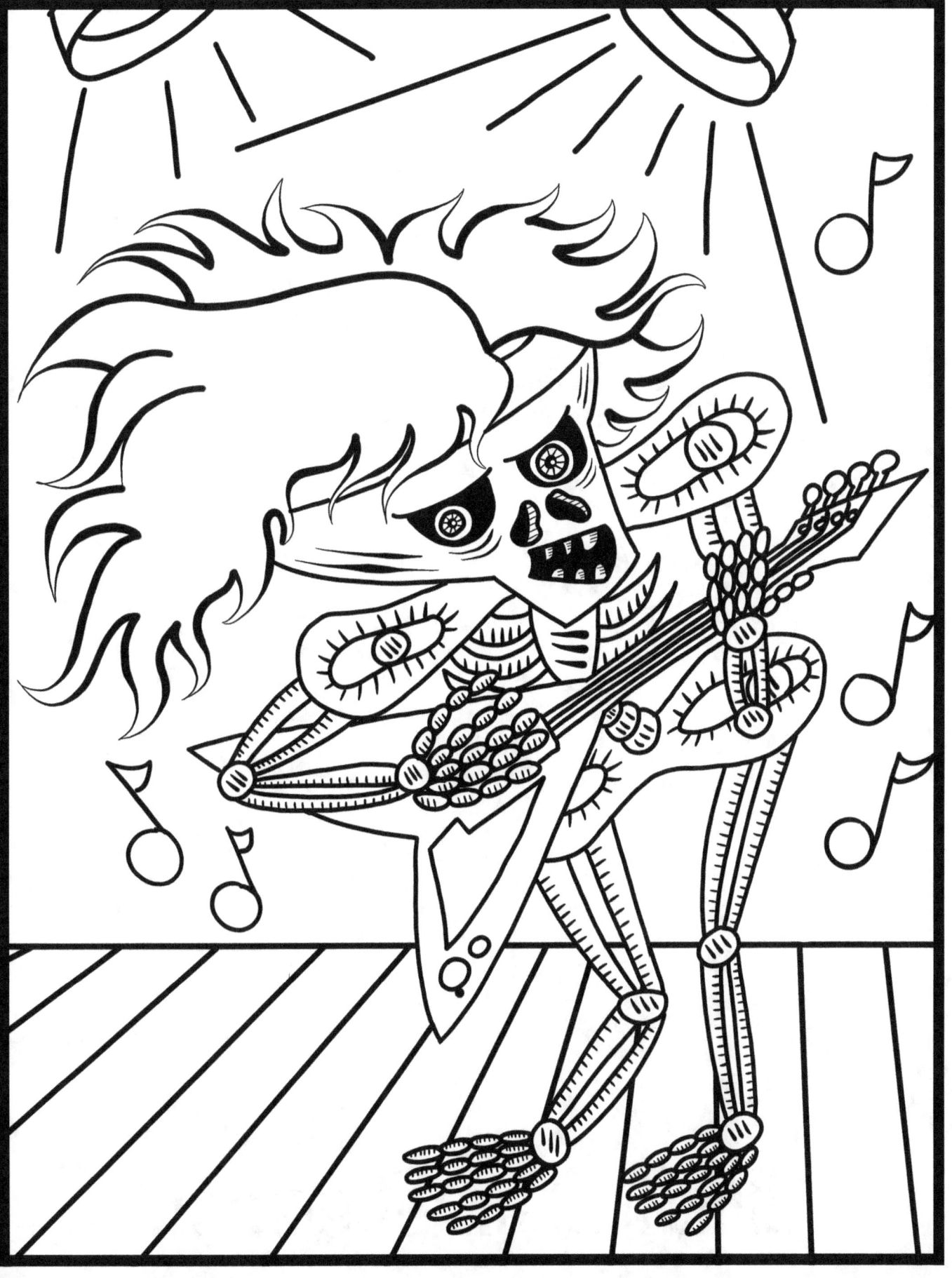

Rock Star Sherman

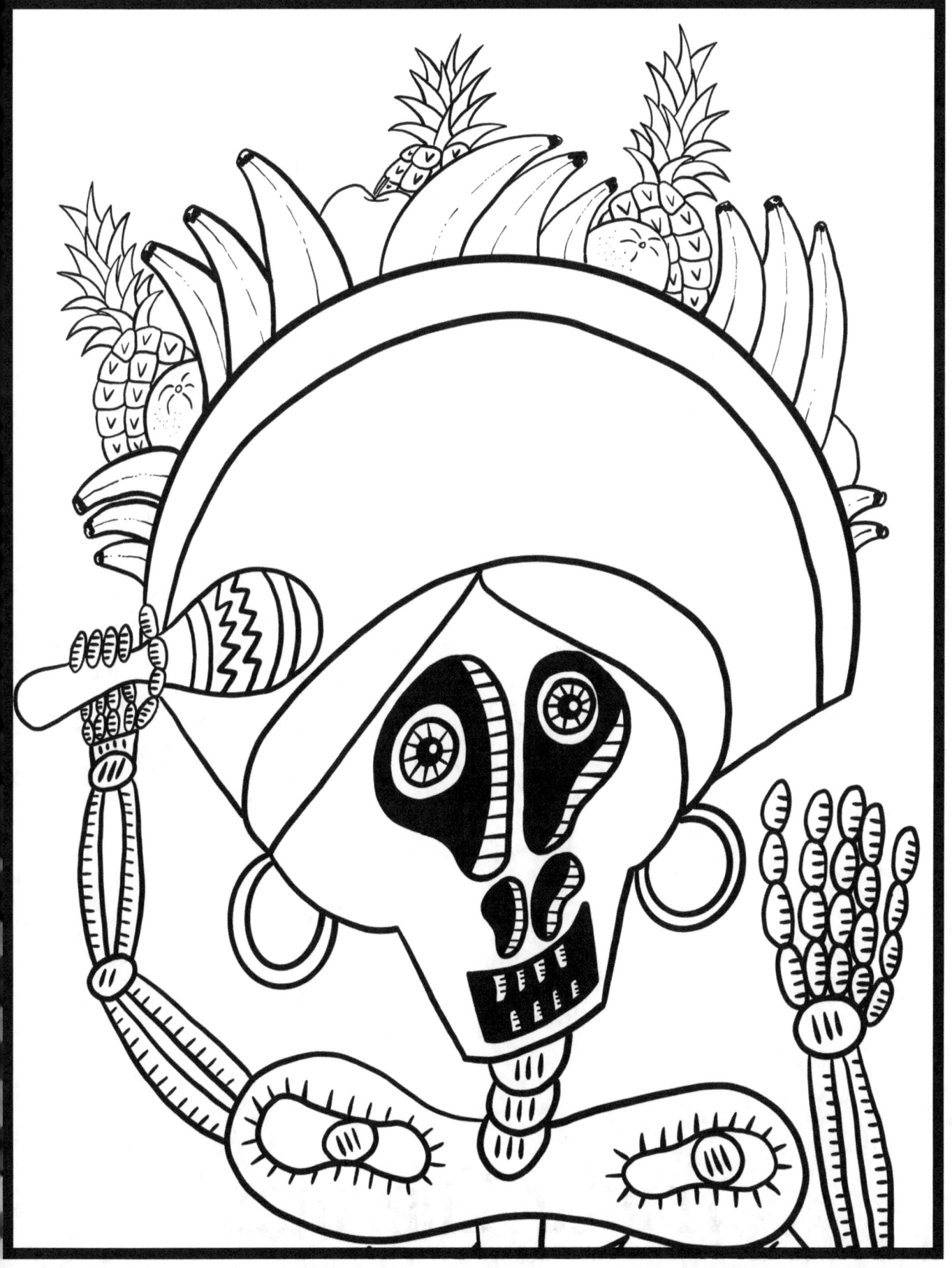

Fruity Sherman

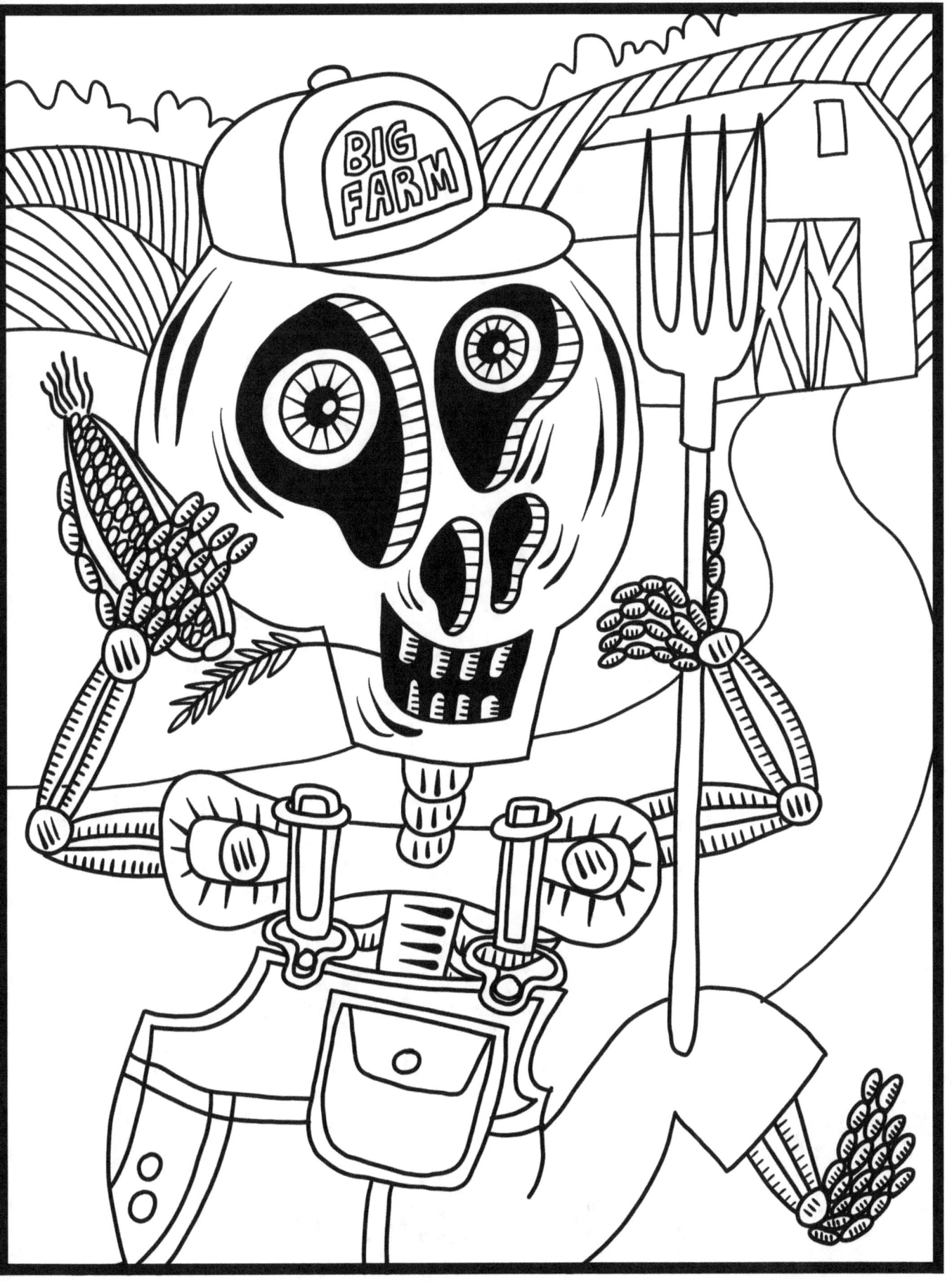

Farmer Sherman

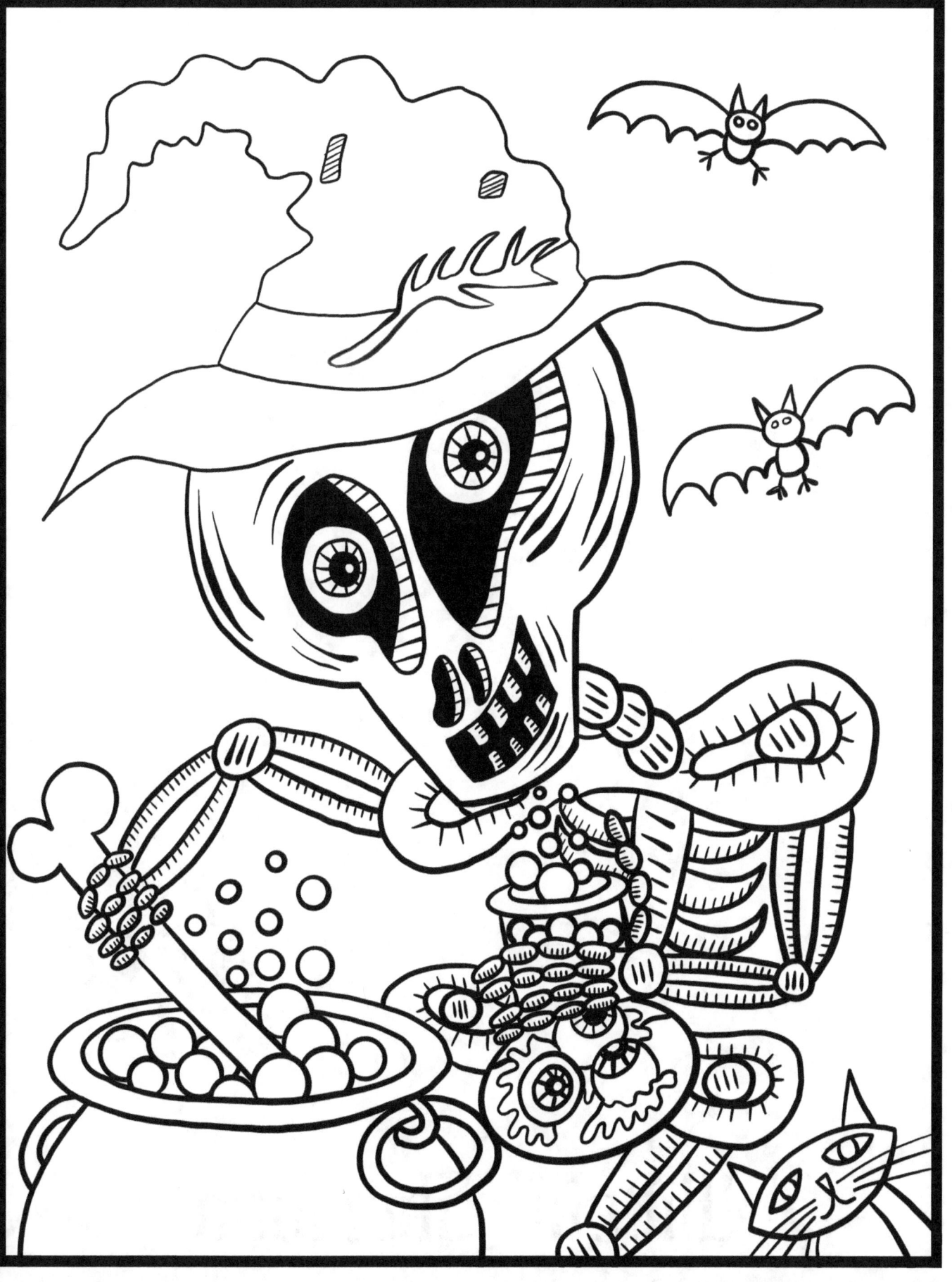

Witchy Sherman

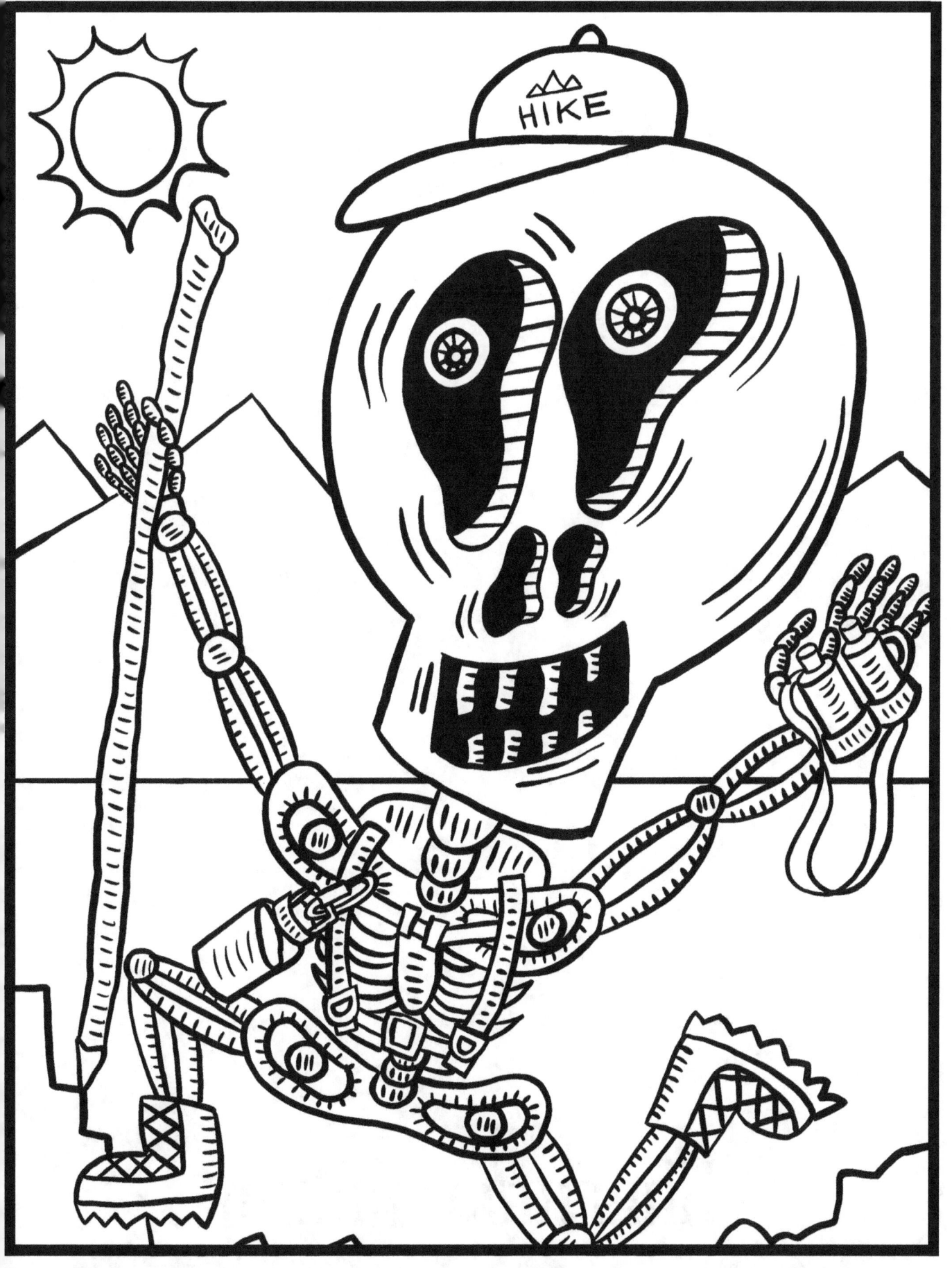

Sherman Hitting

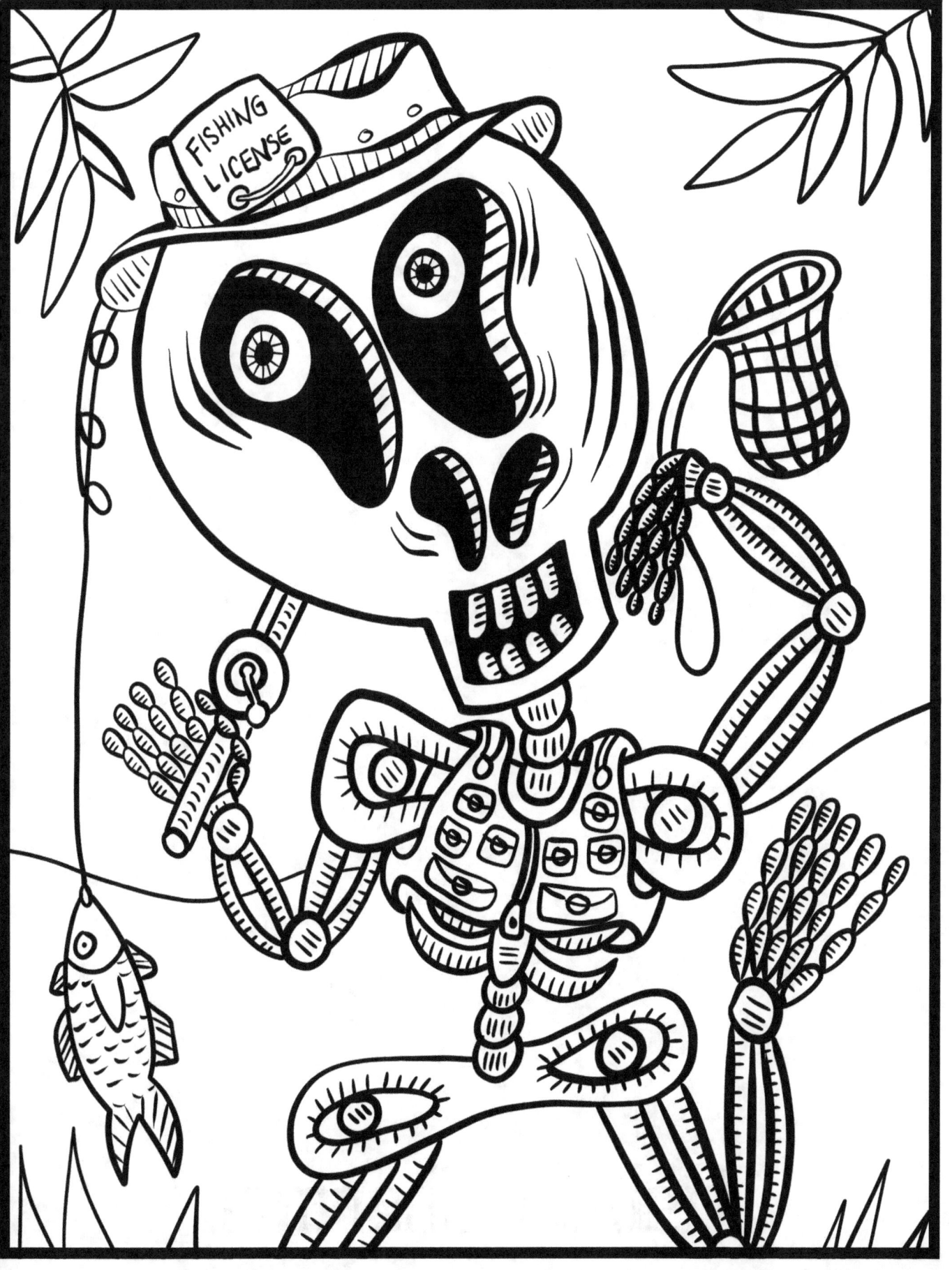

Fishing Sherman

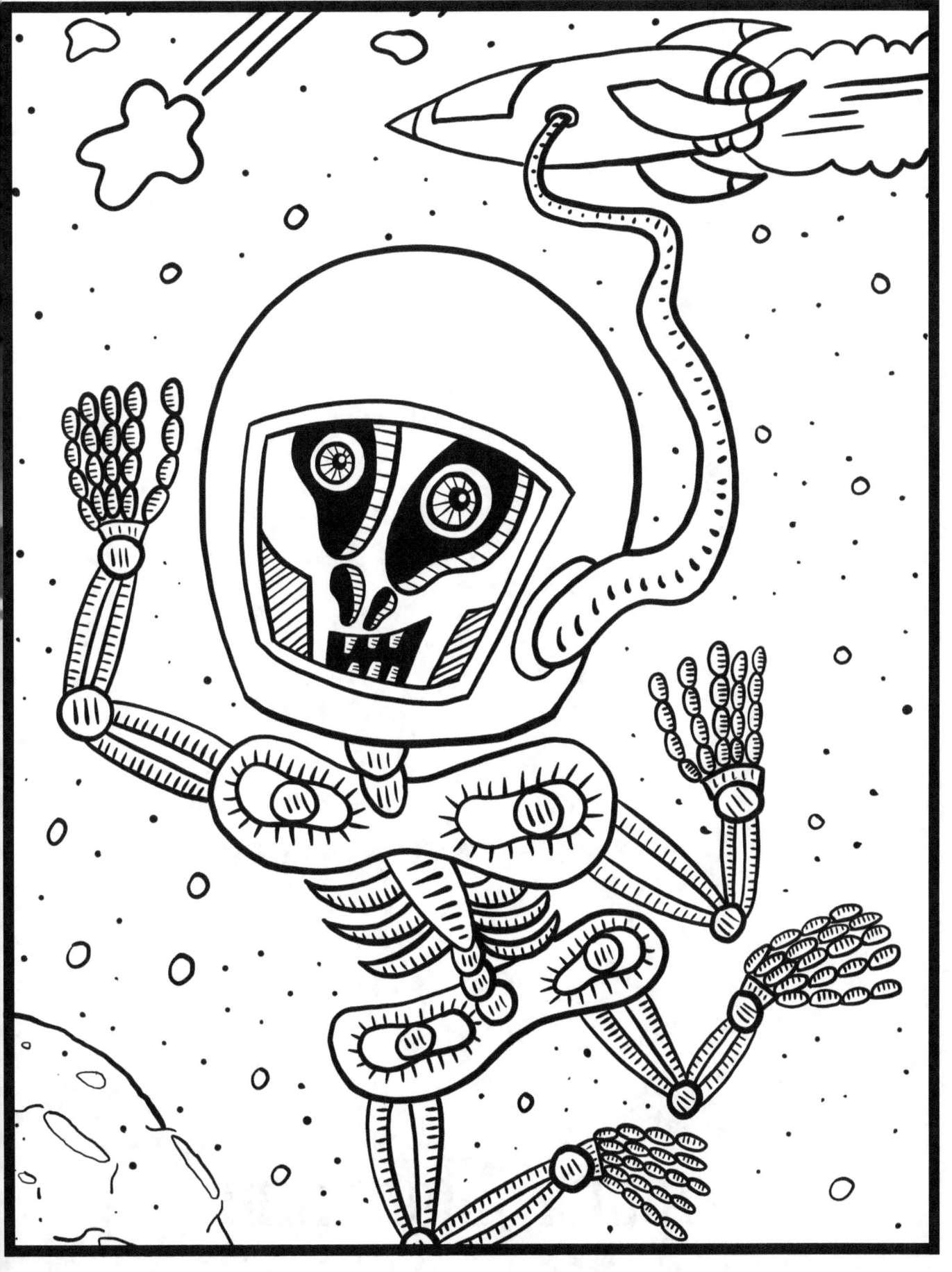

Space Sherman

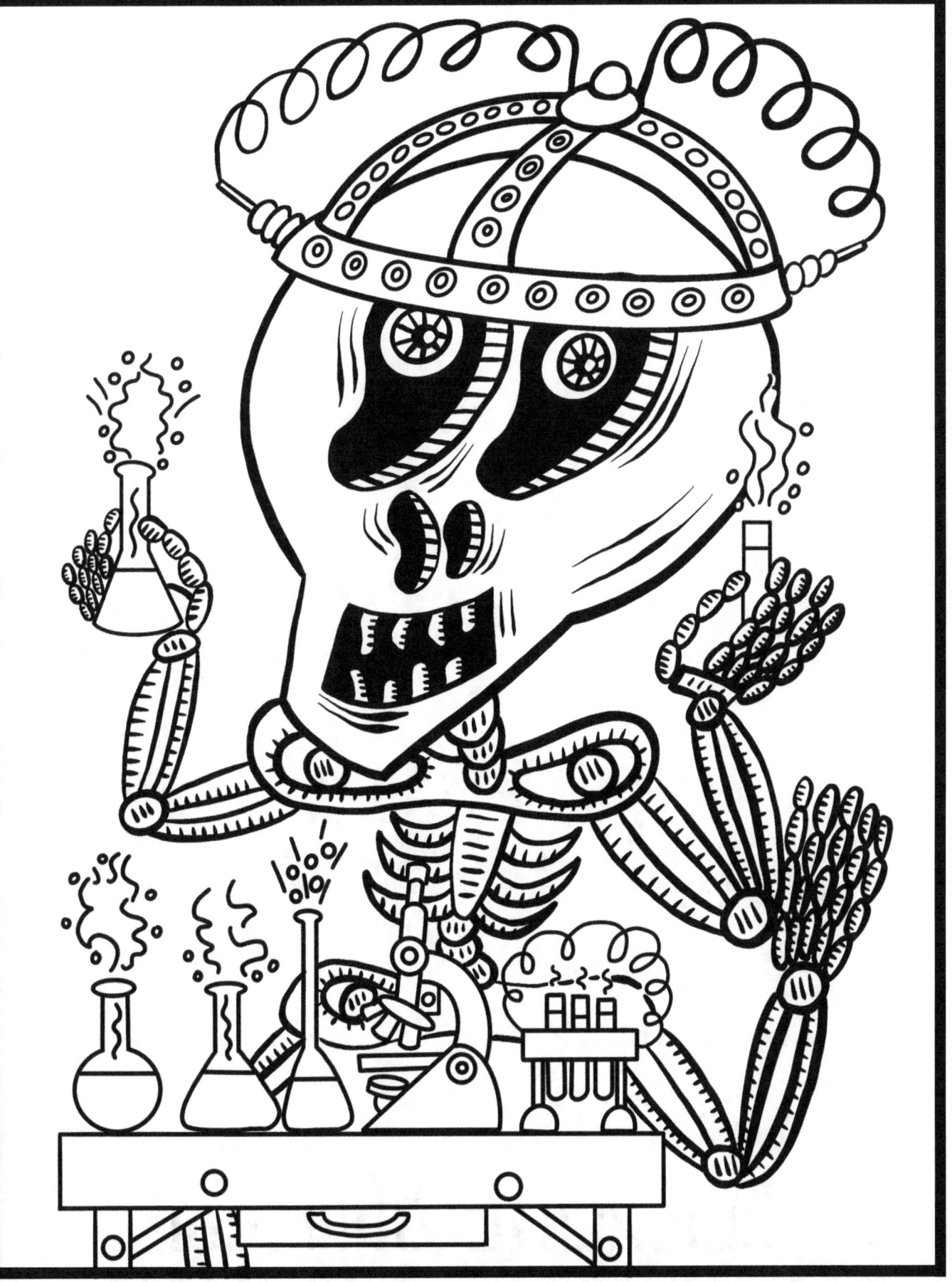

Scientific Sherman

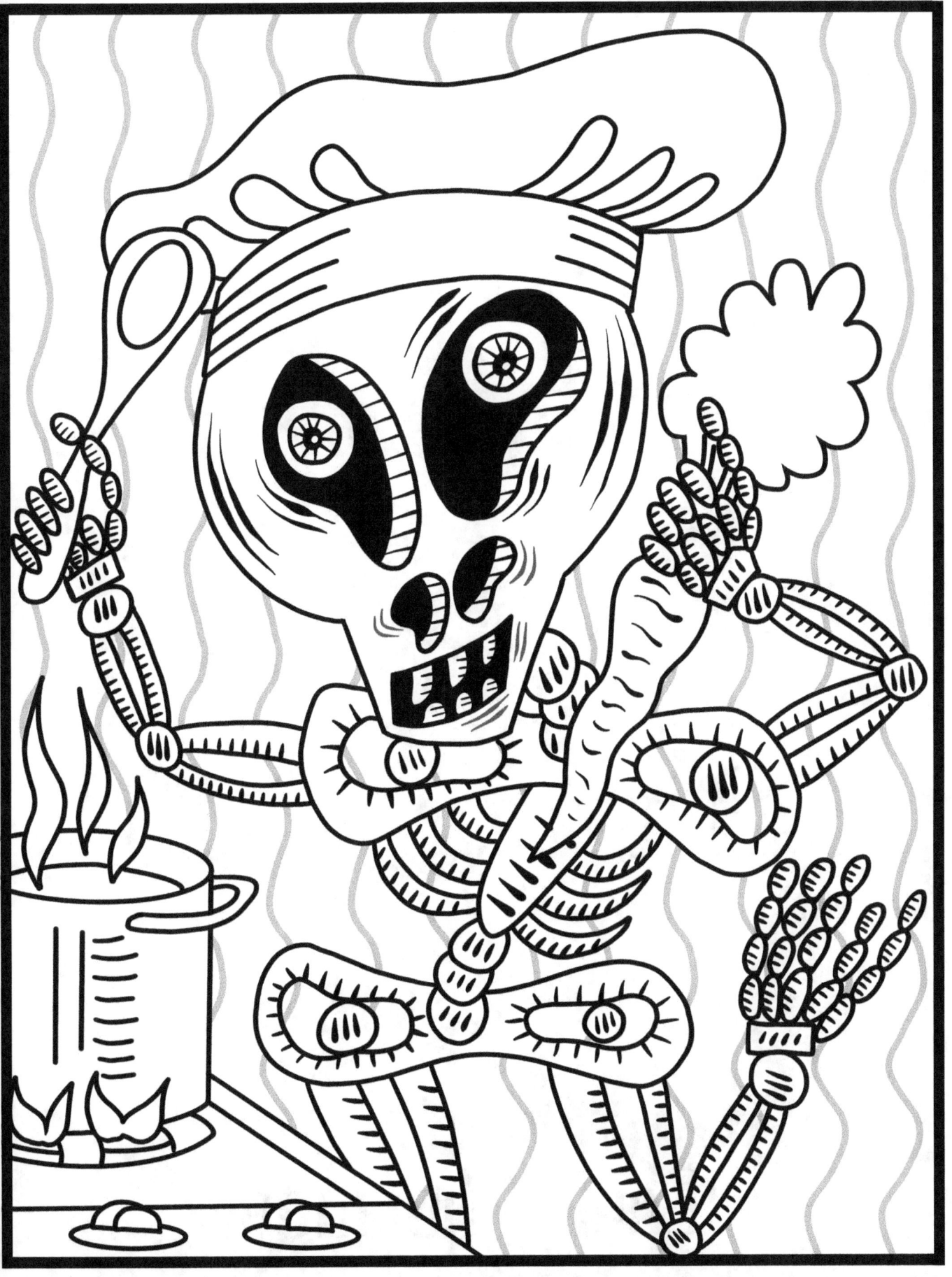

Chef Sherman

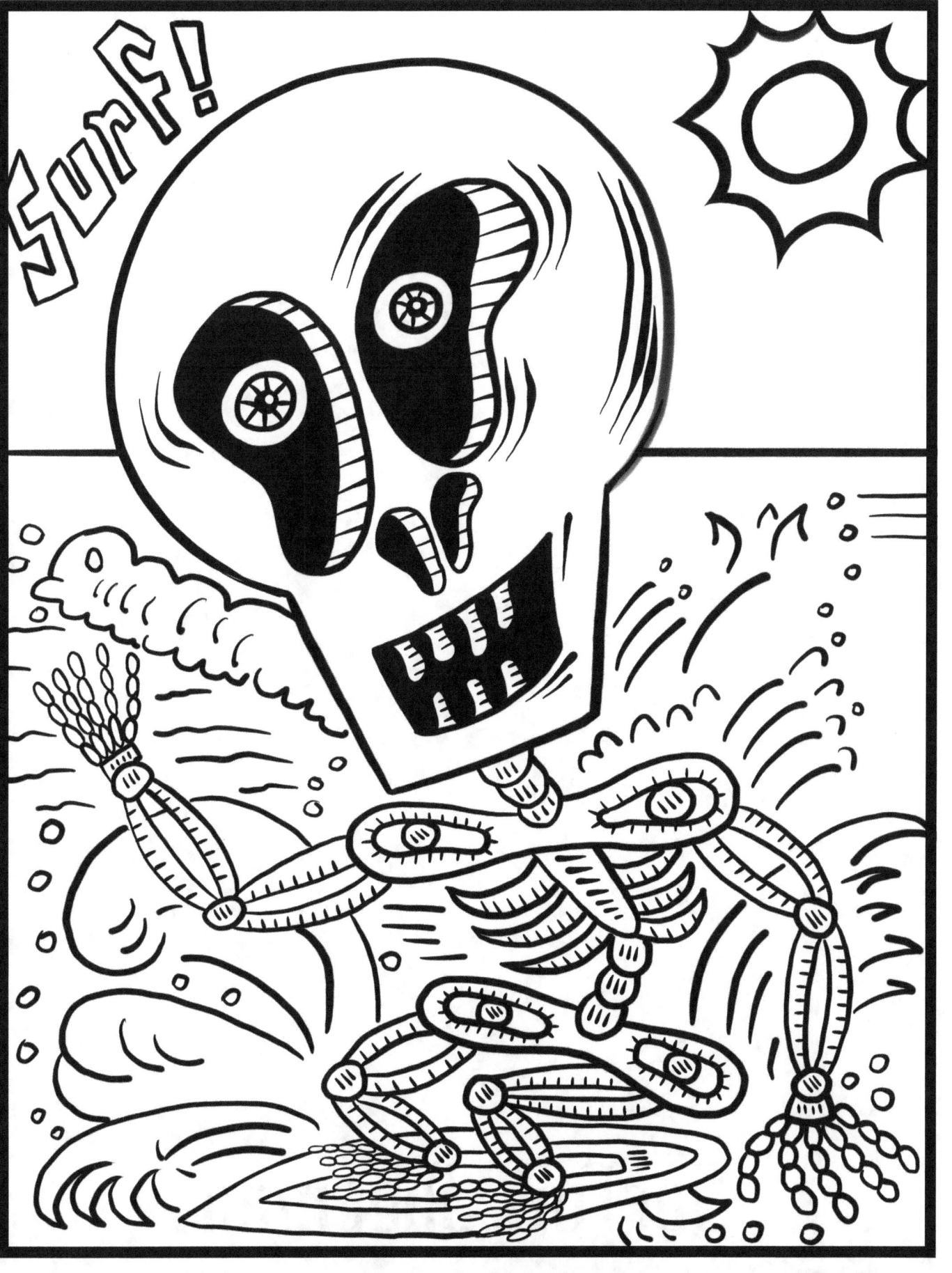

Surfin' Sherman

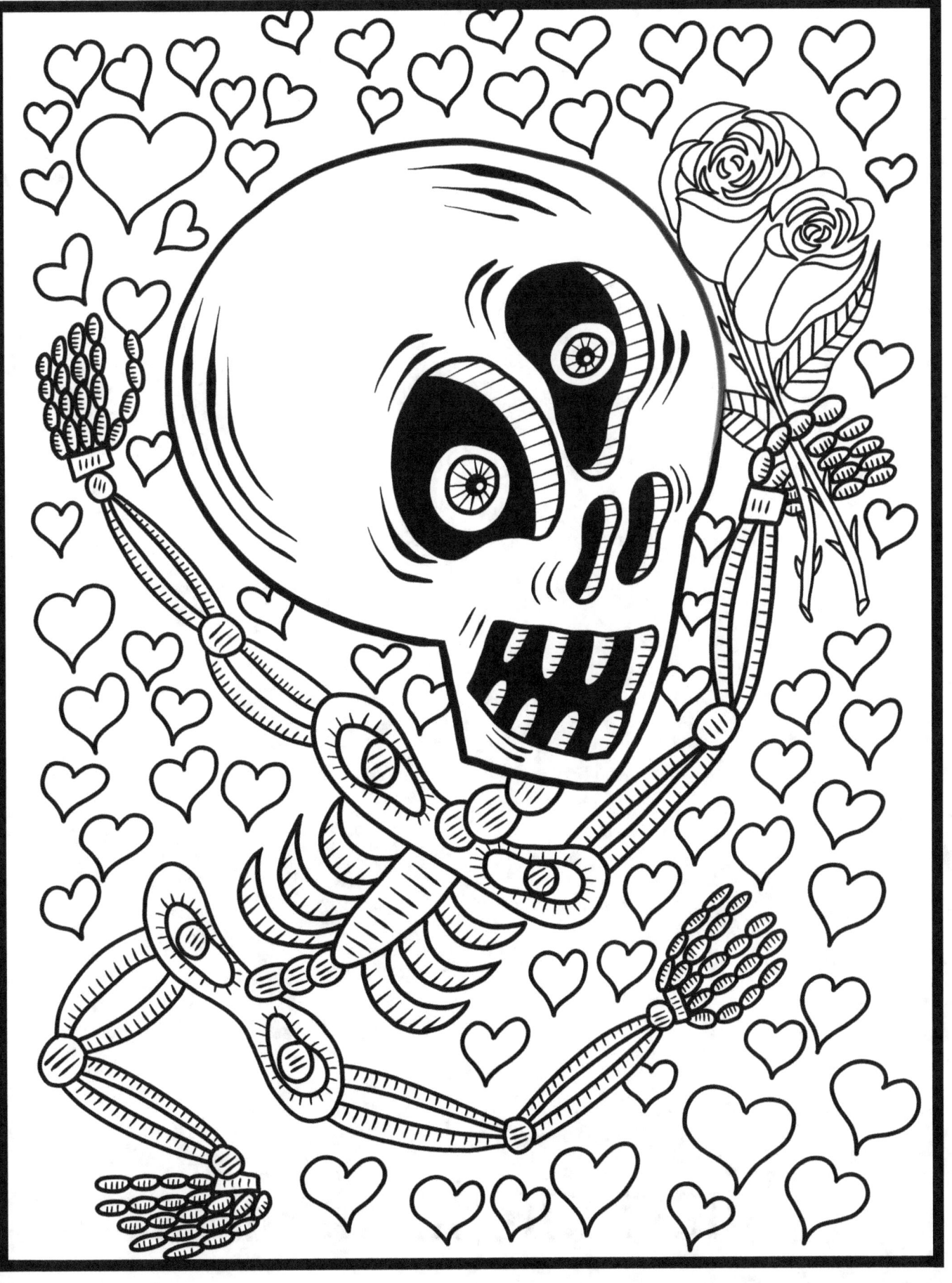

Sherman in Hearts

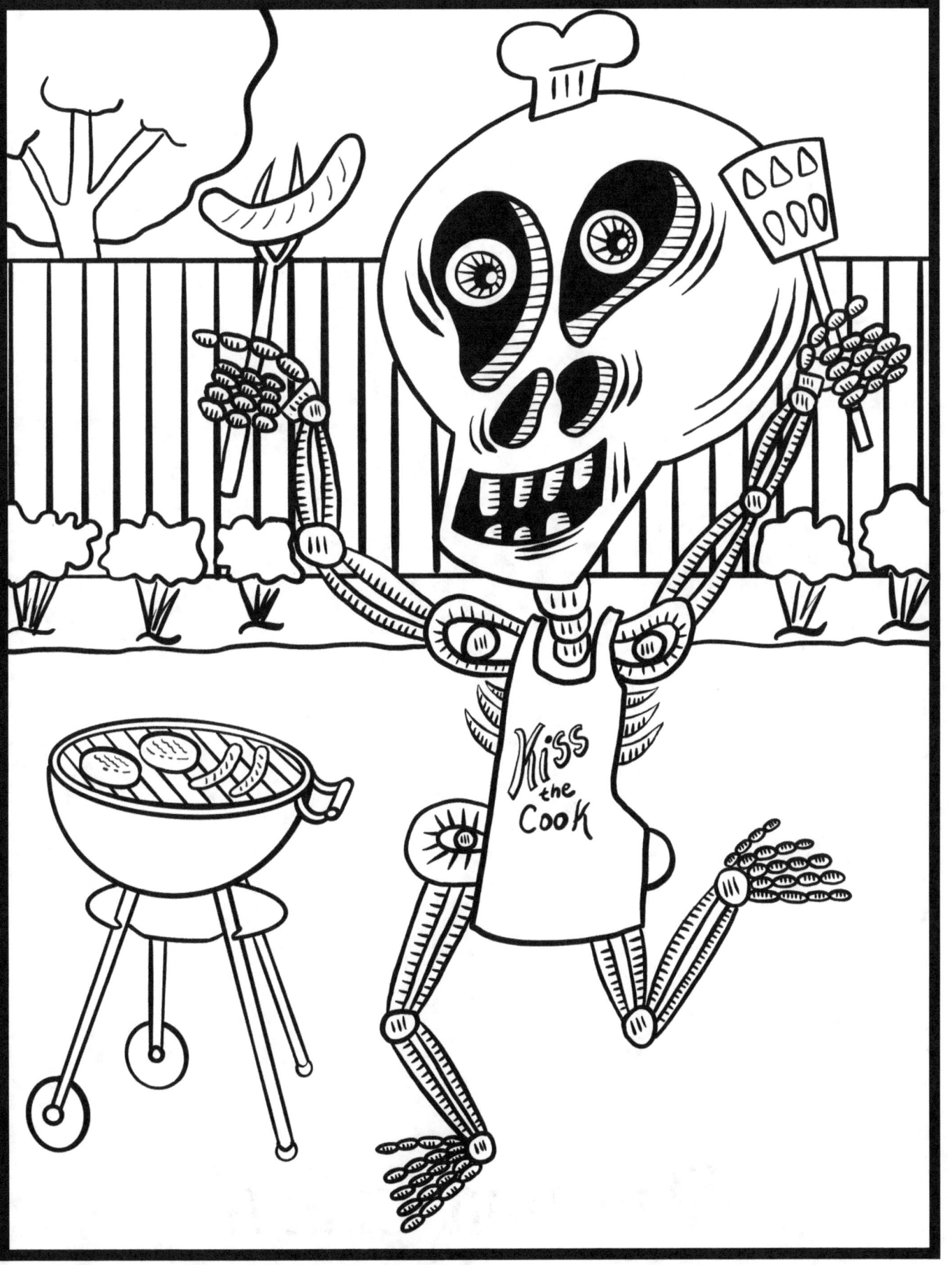

Sherman Grillin'

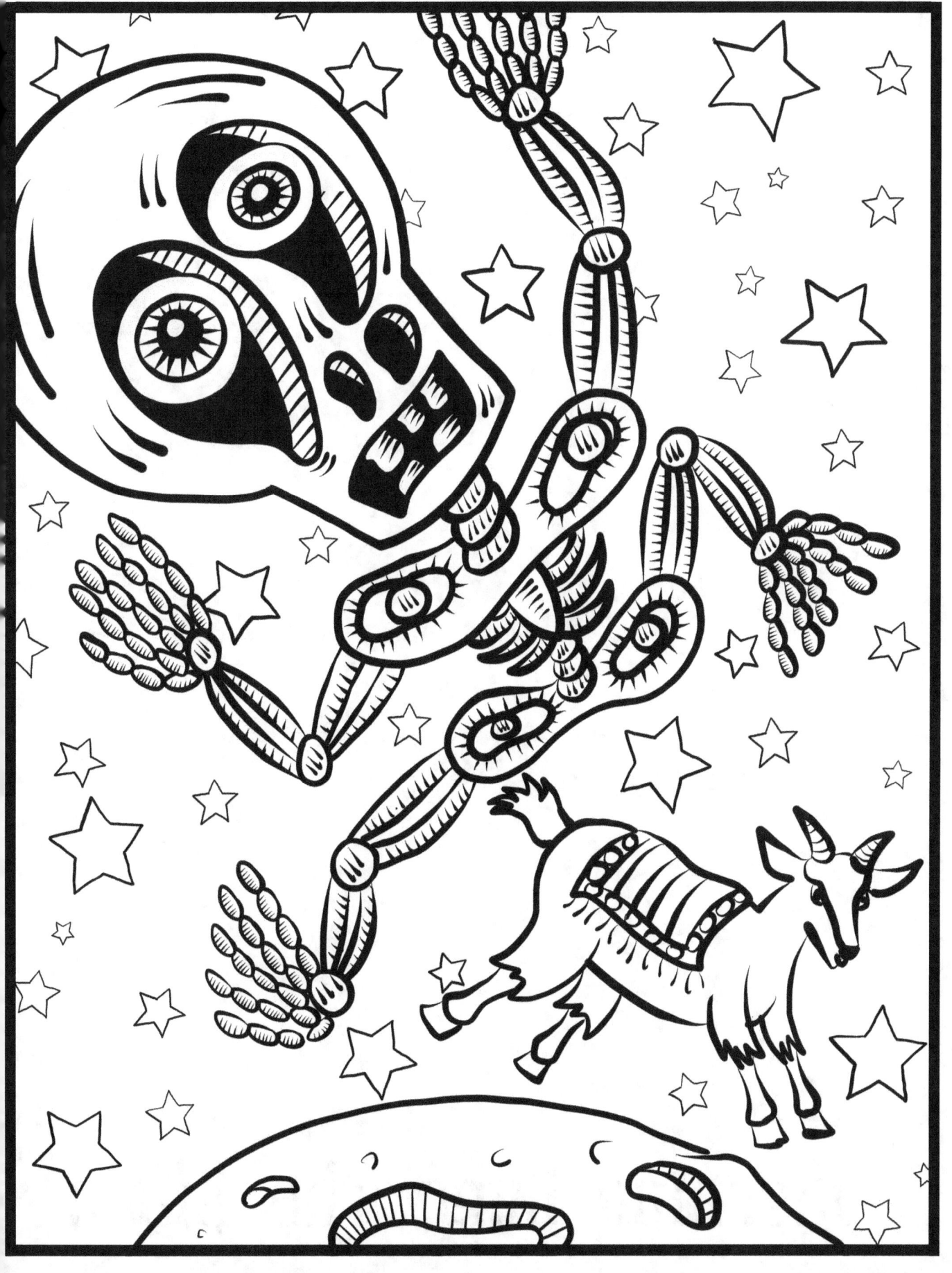

Sherman Over The Moon

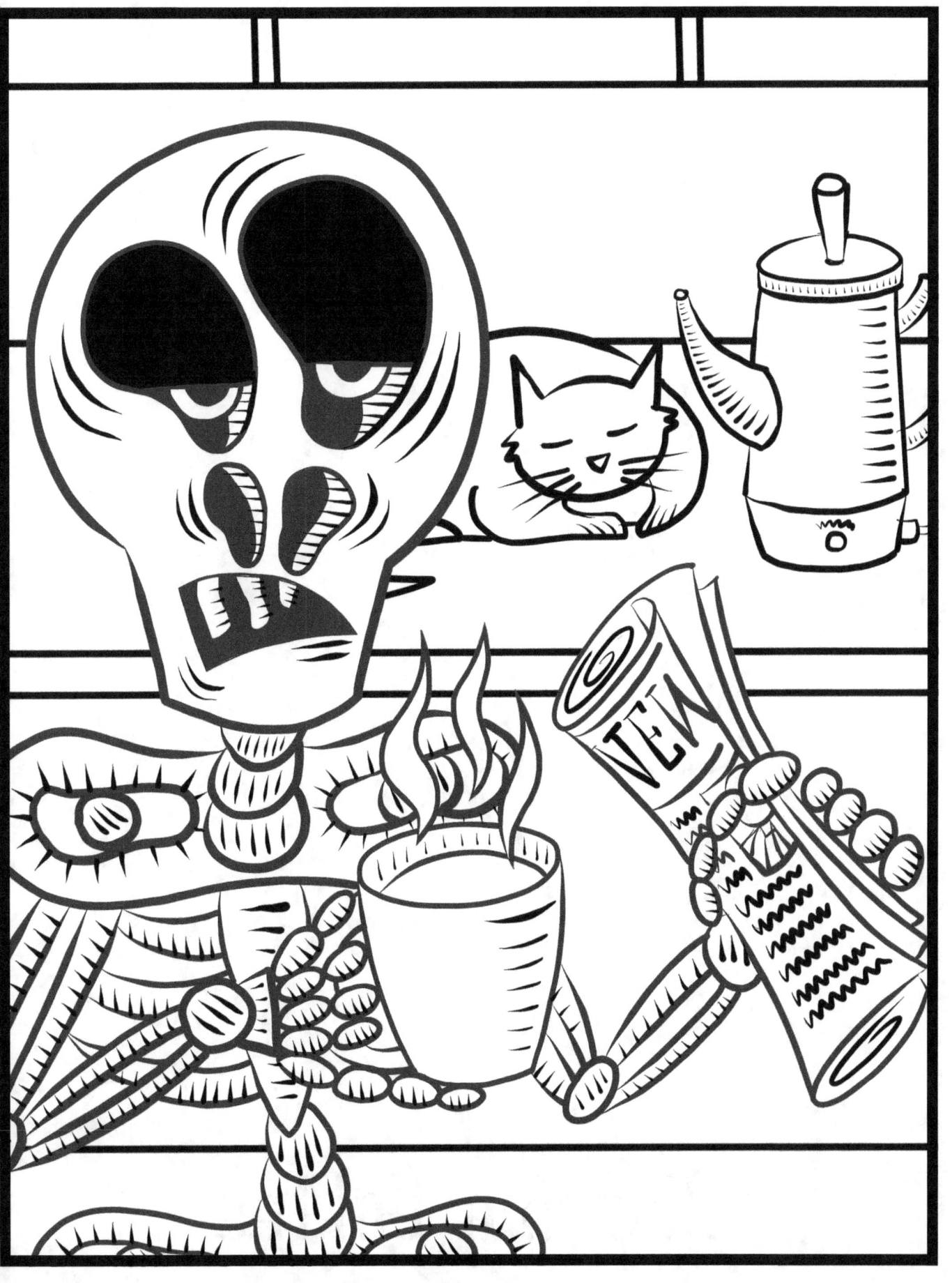

Morning Coffee

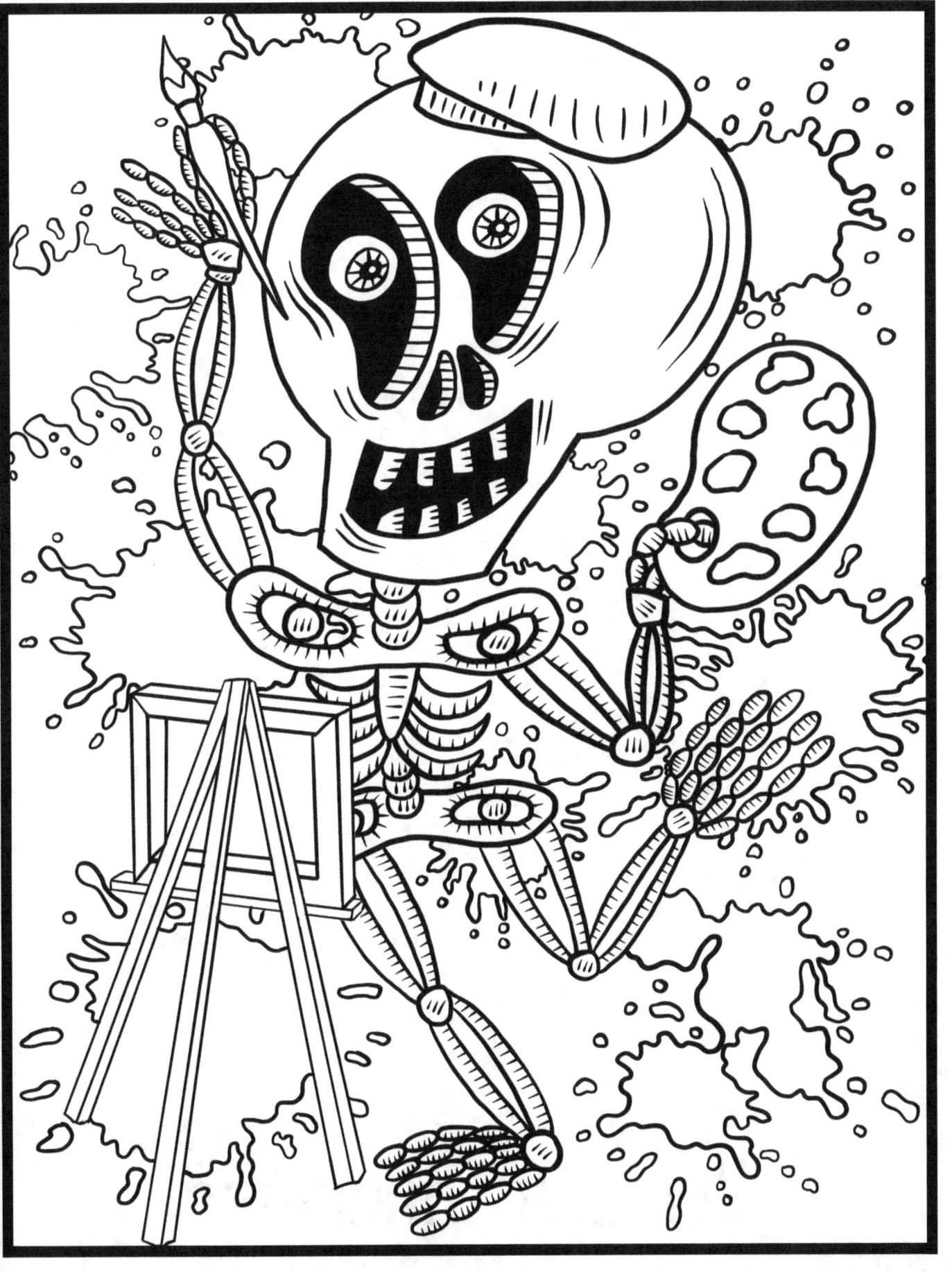

Artistic Sherman

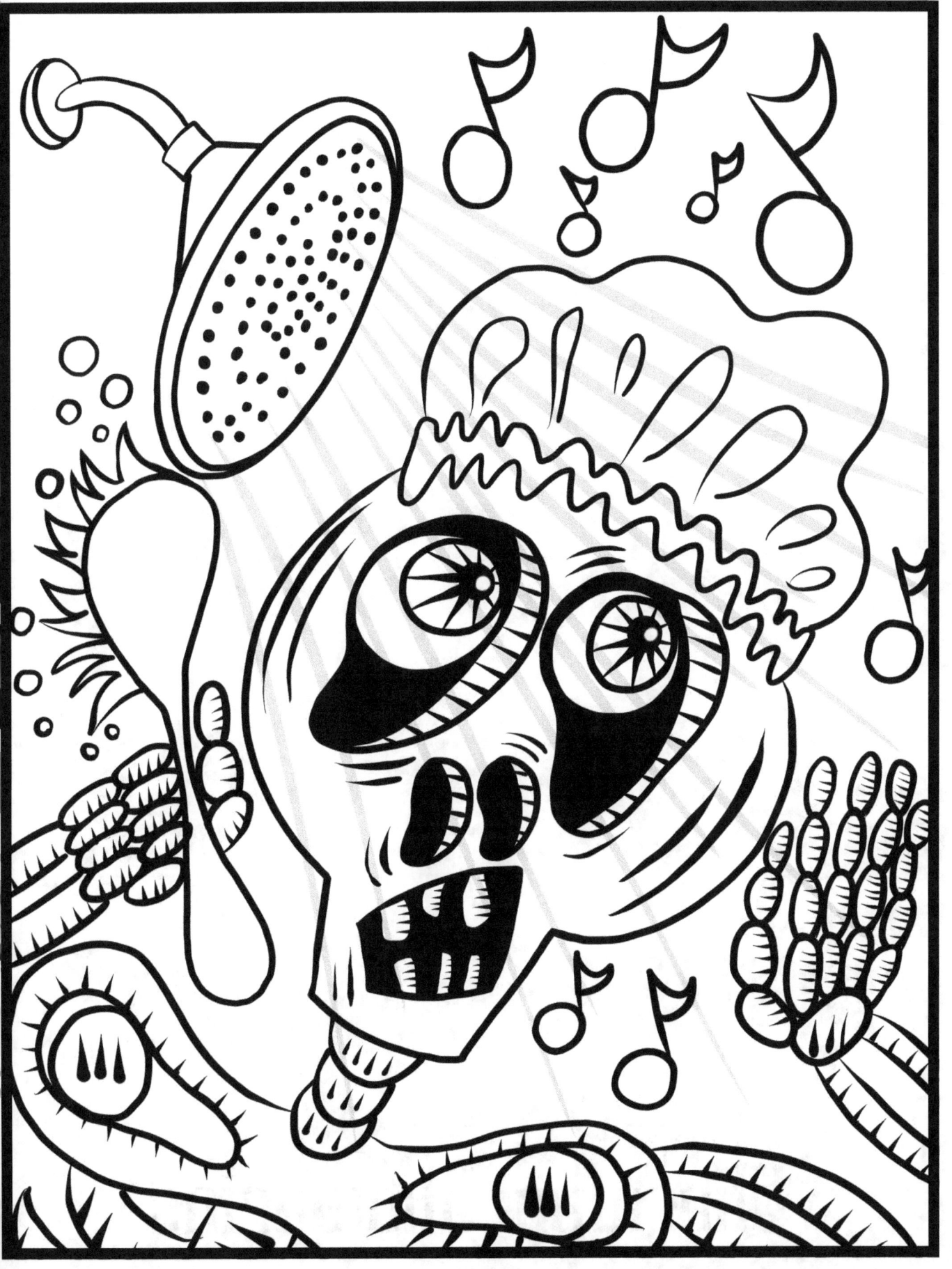

Sherman Showering

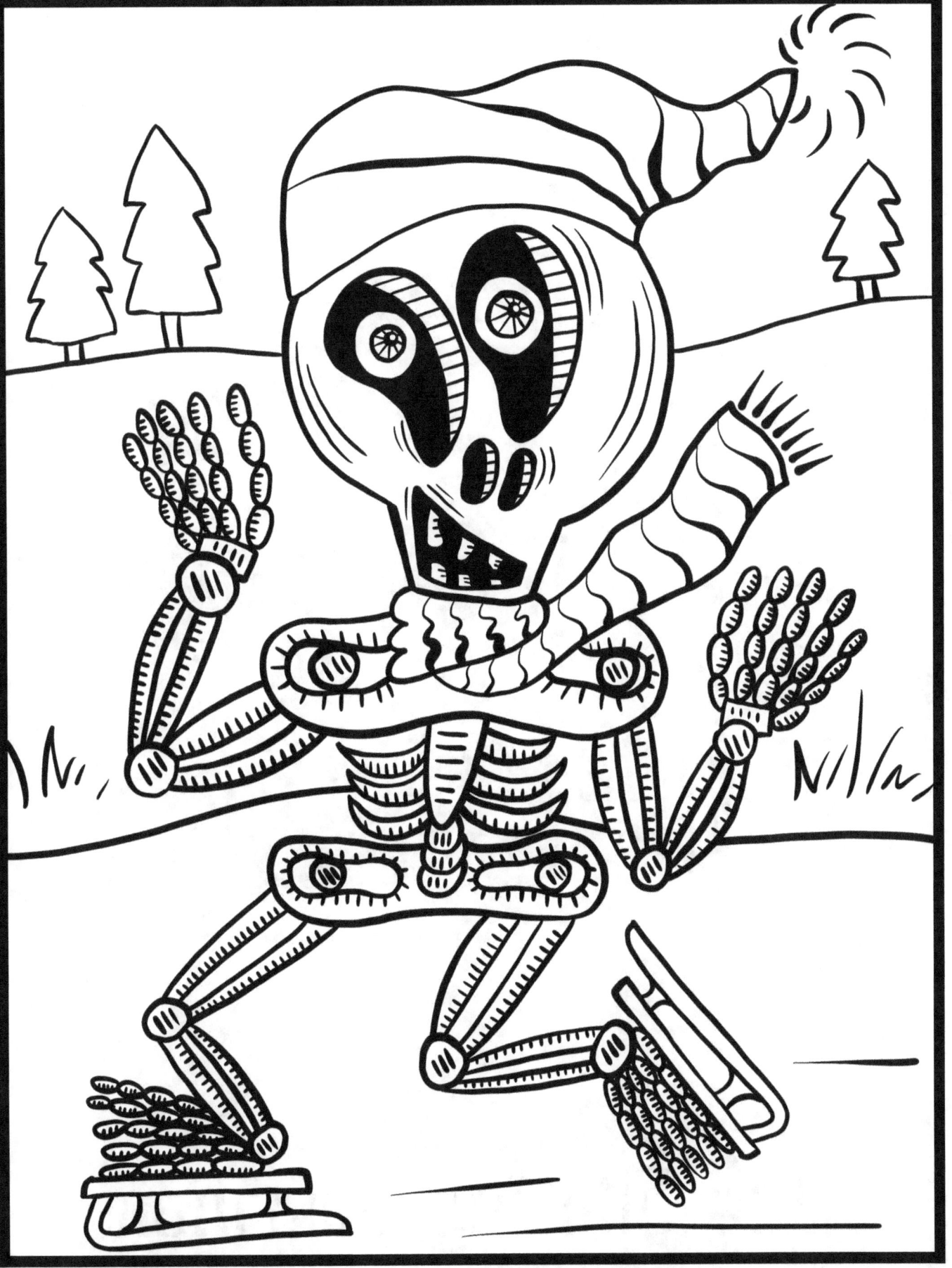

Ice Skating Sherman

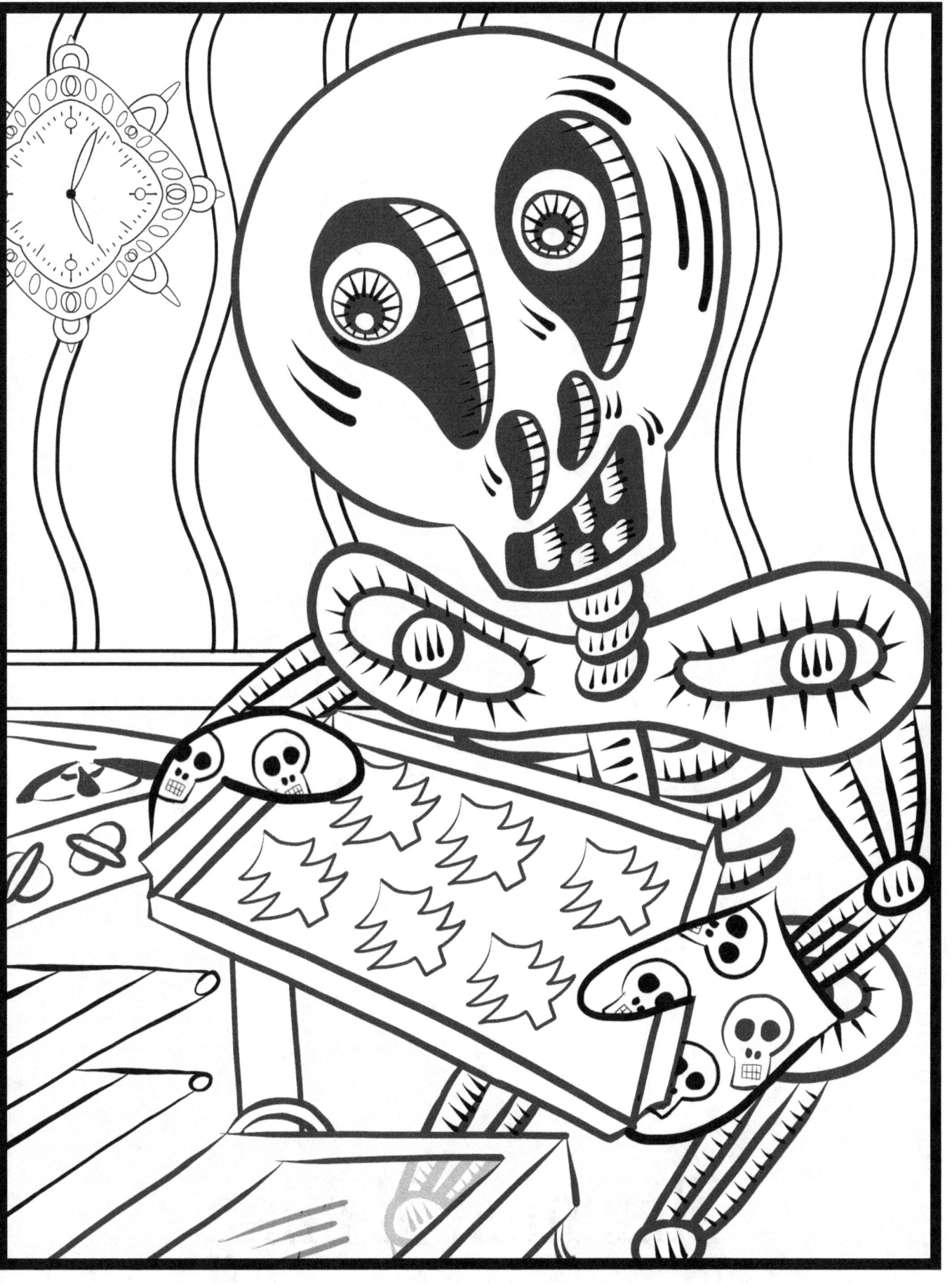

Sherman Balting

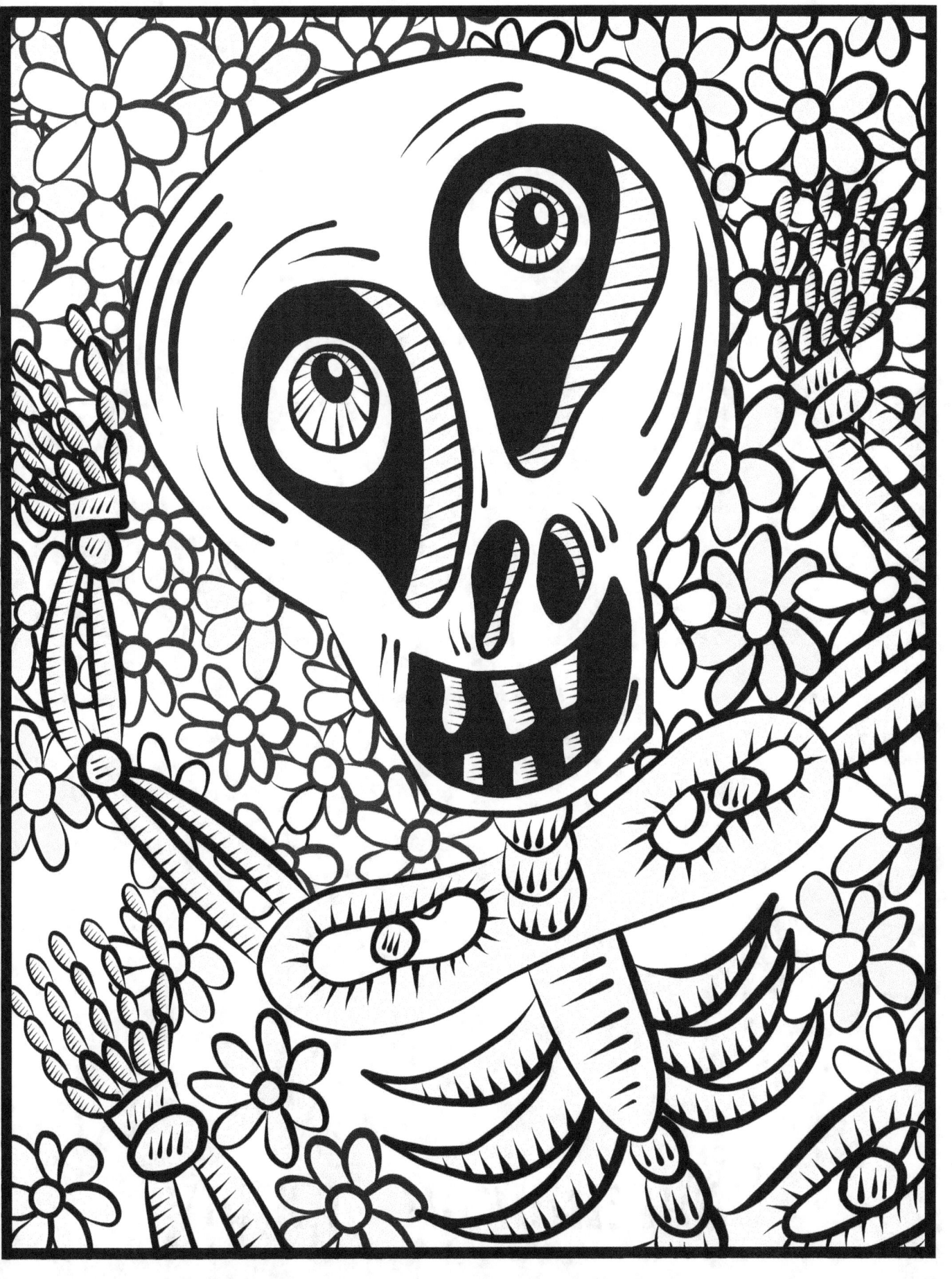

Sherman in Spring

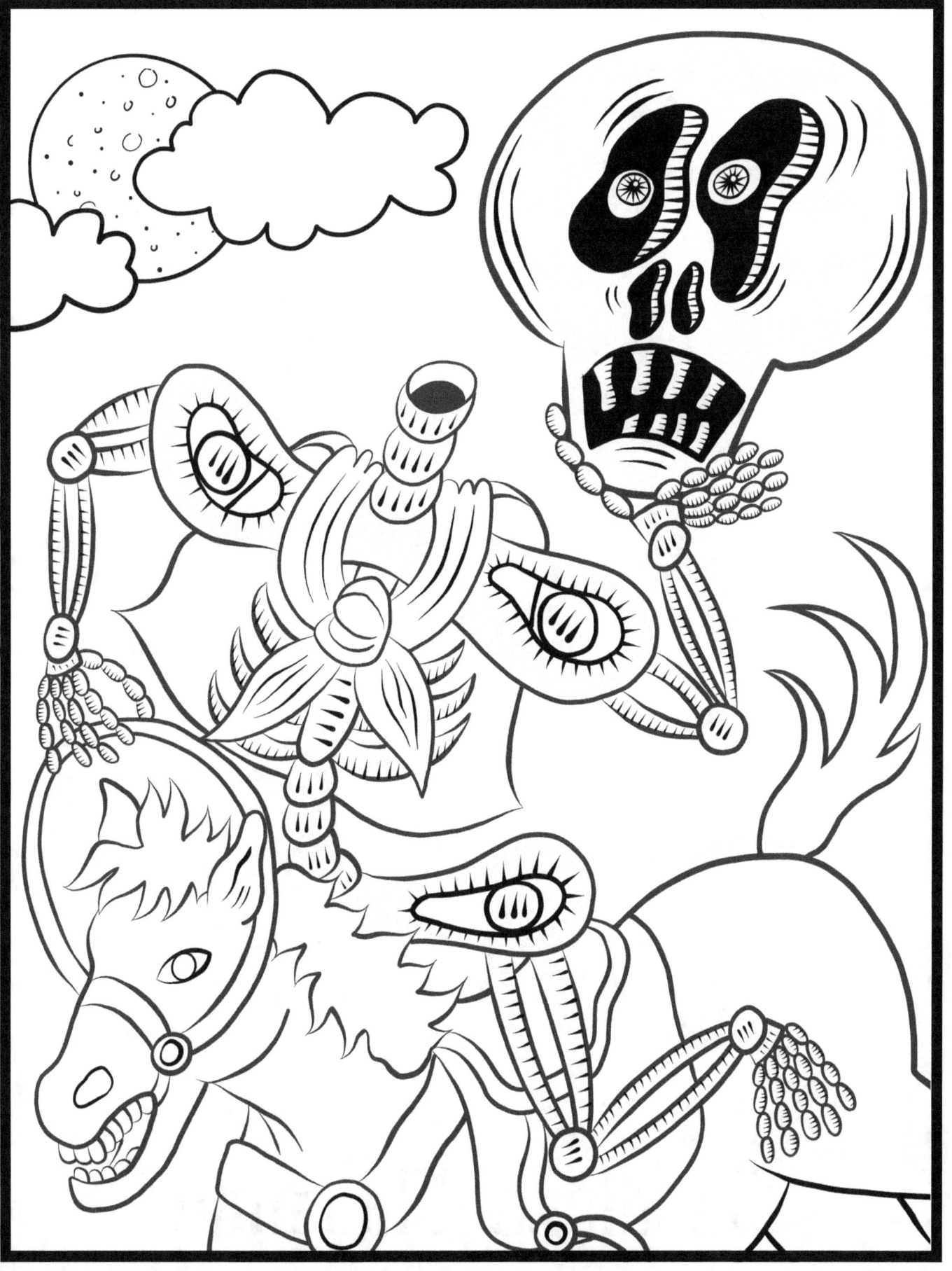

Headless Sherman

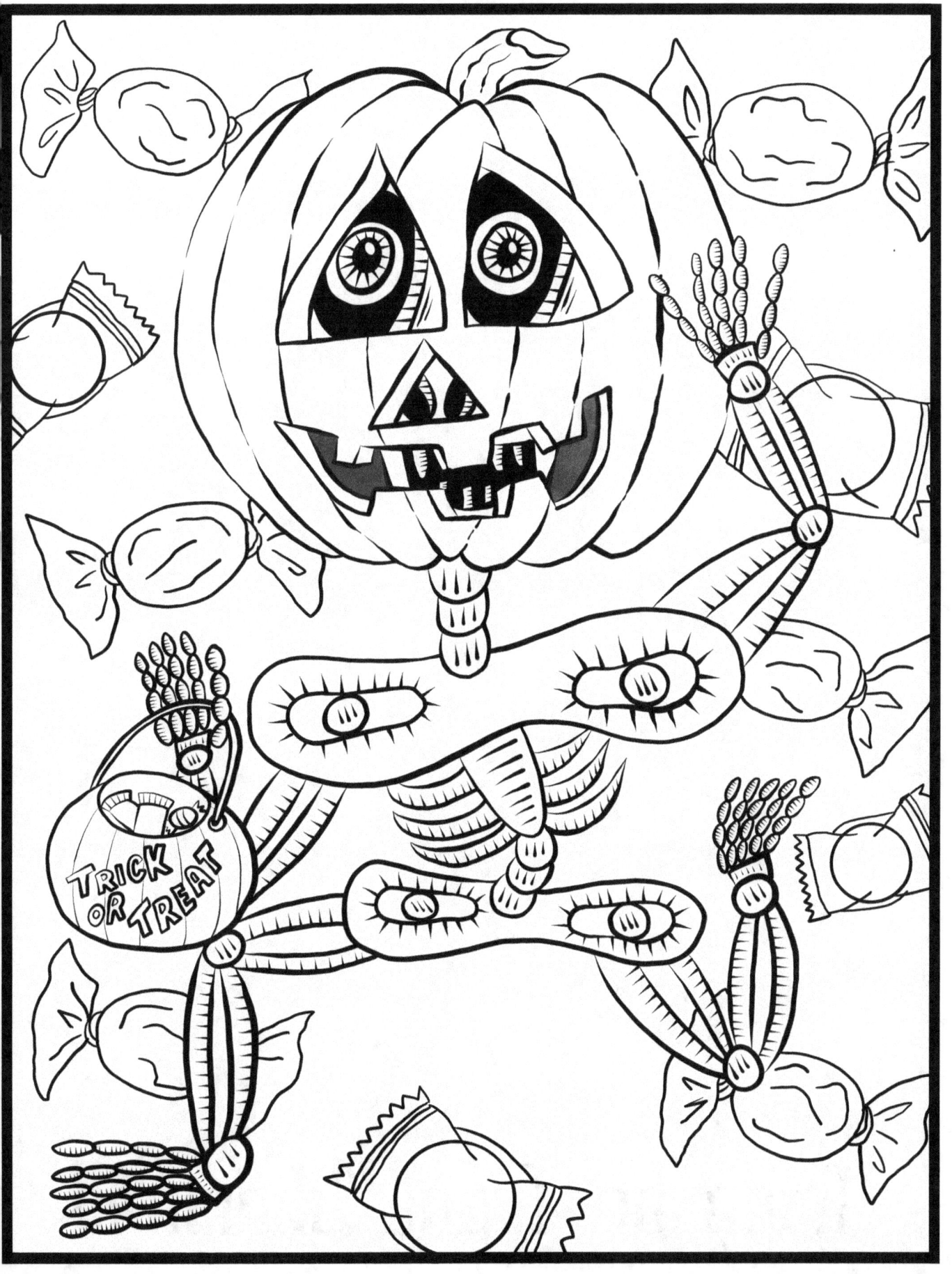

Trick or Treat Sherman

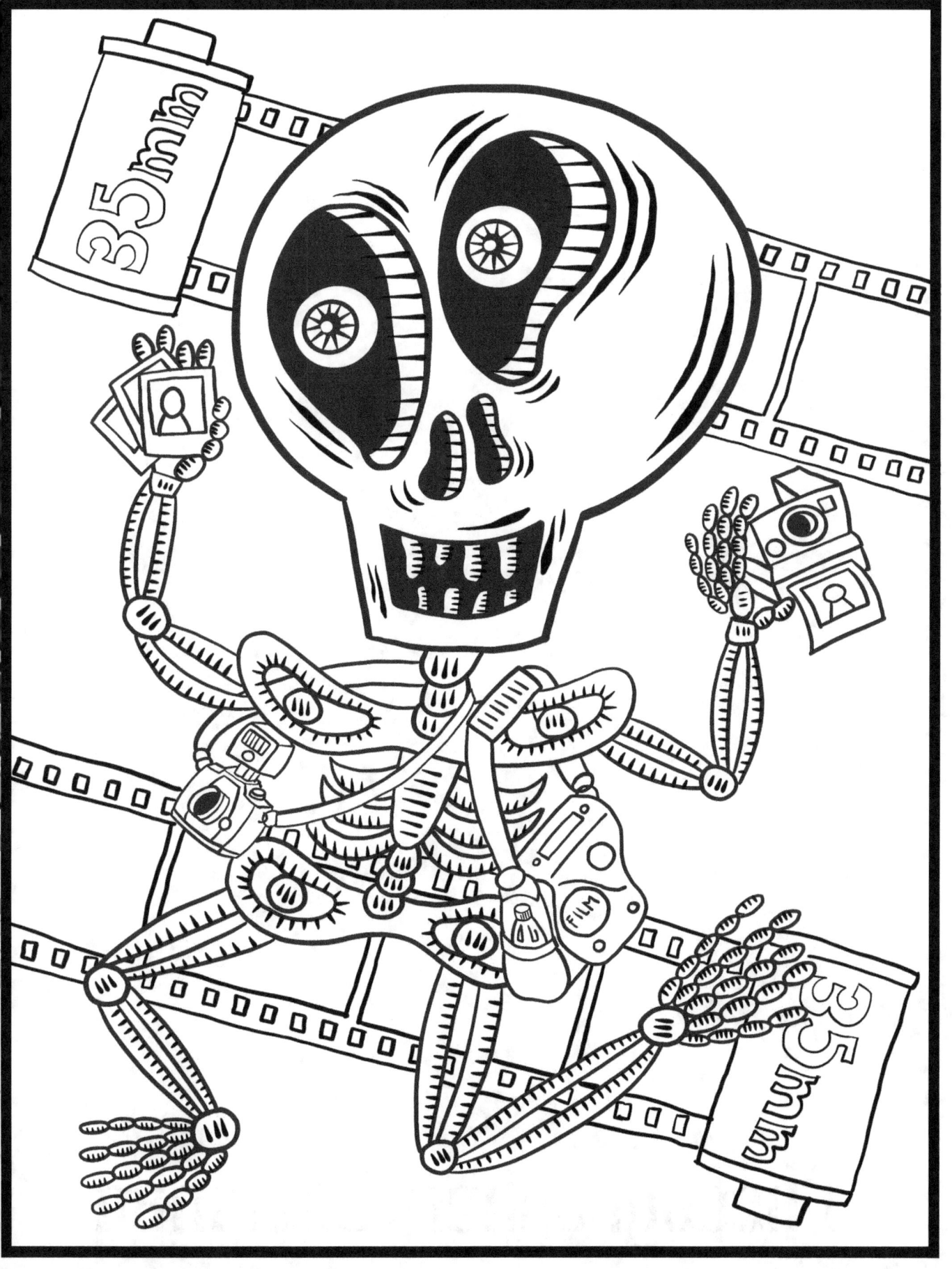

Photographer Sherman

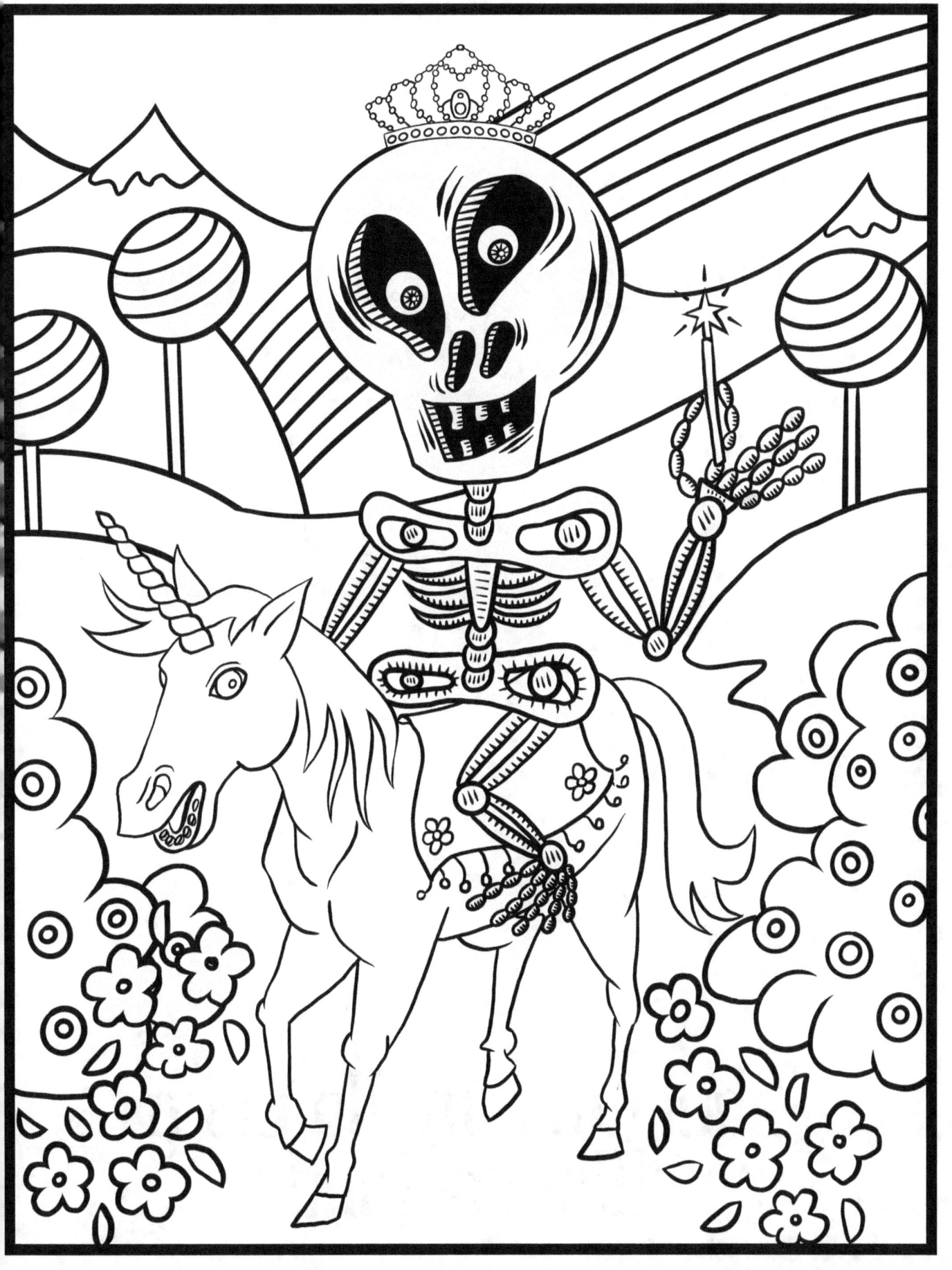

Sherman in Unicorn Wonderland

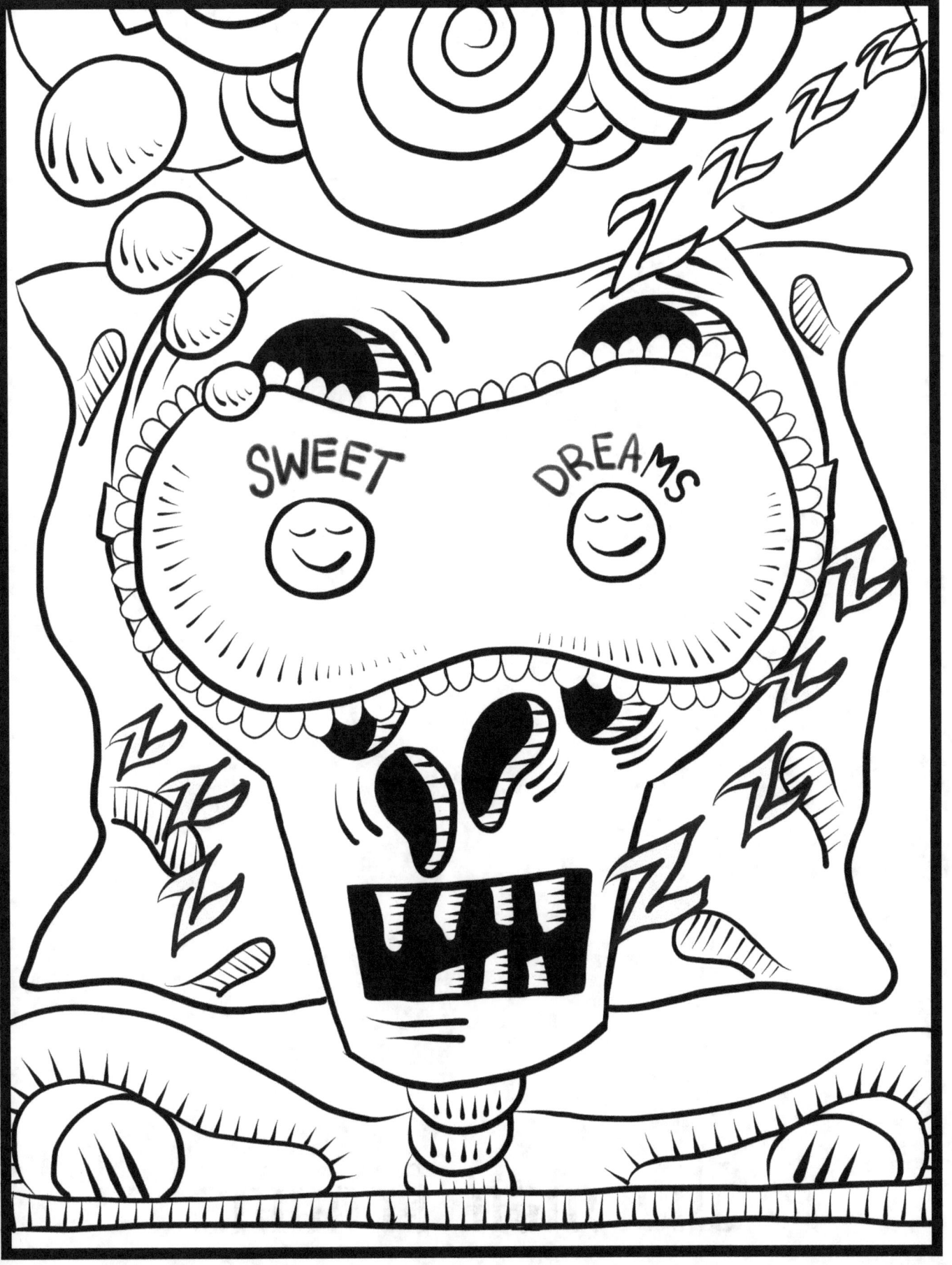

Sherman Dreams

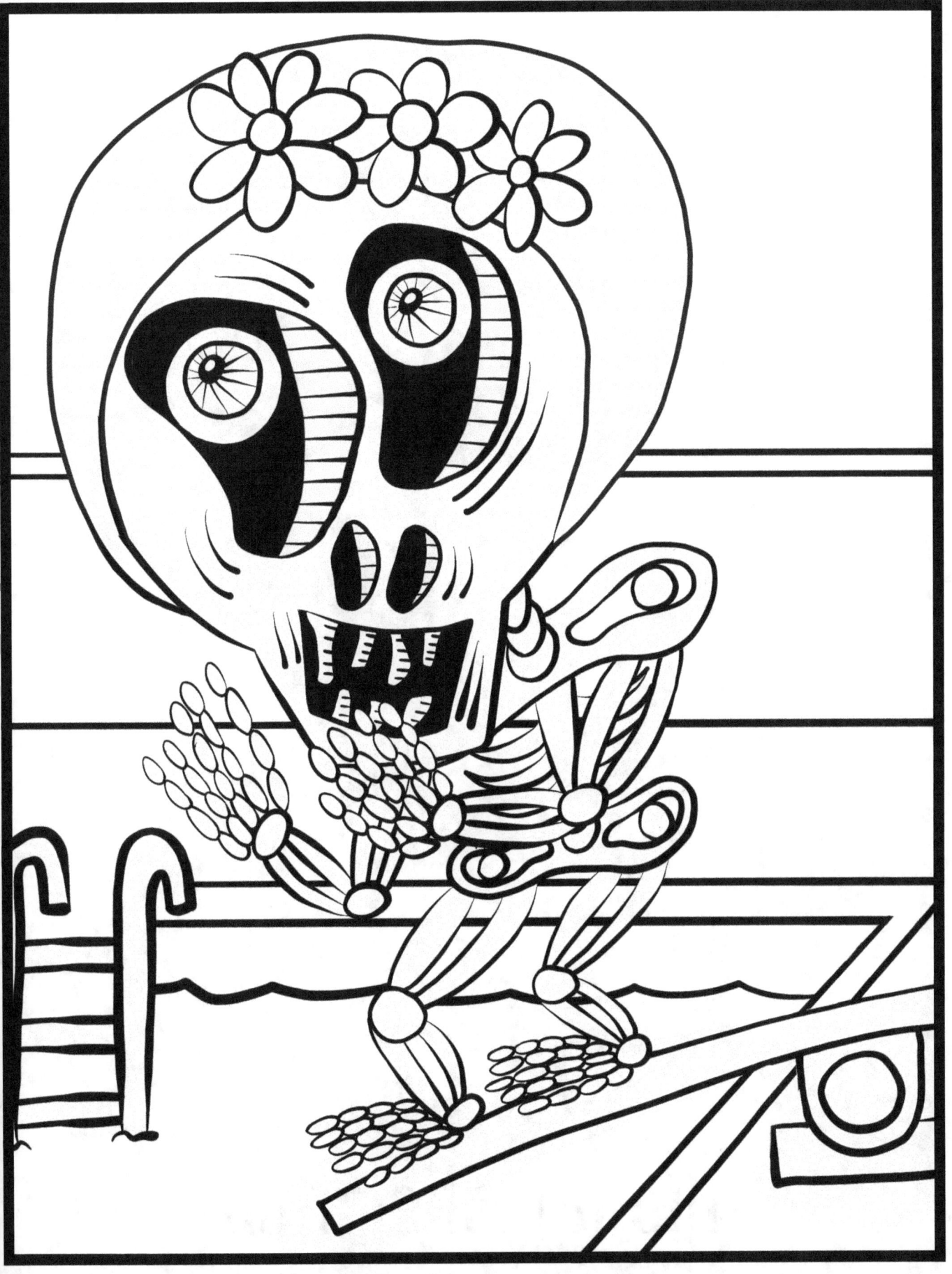

Diving Sherman

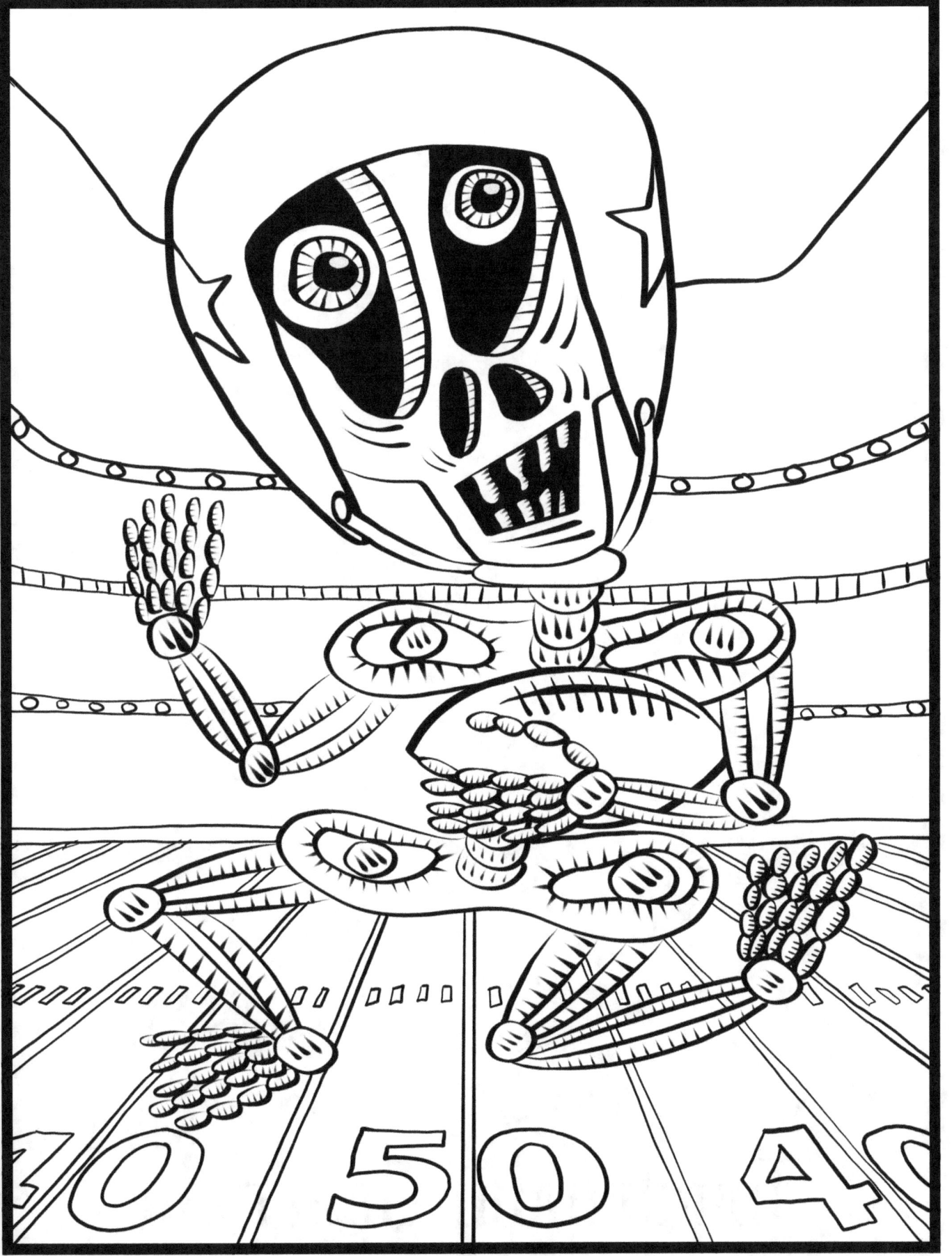

Touchdown Sherman

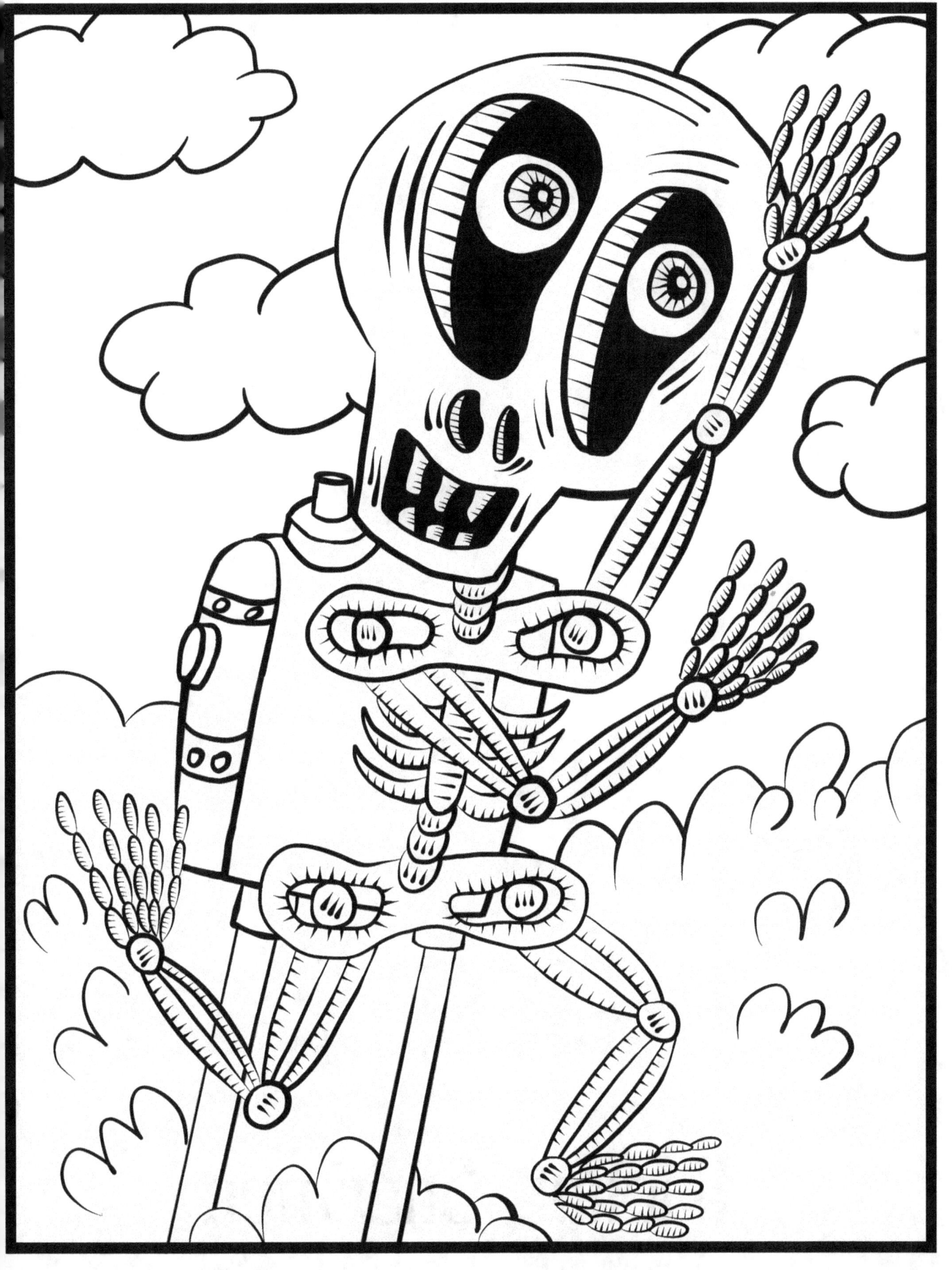

Rocket Sherman

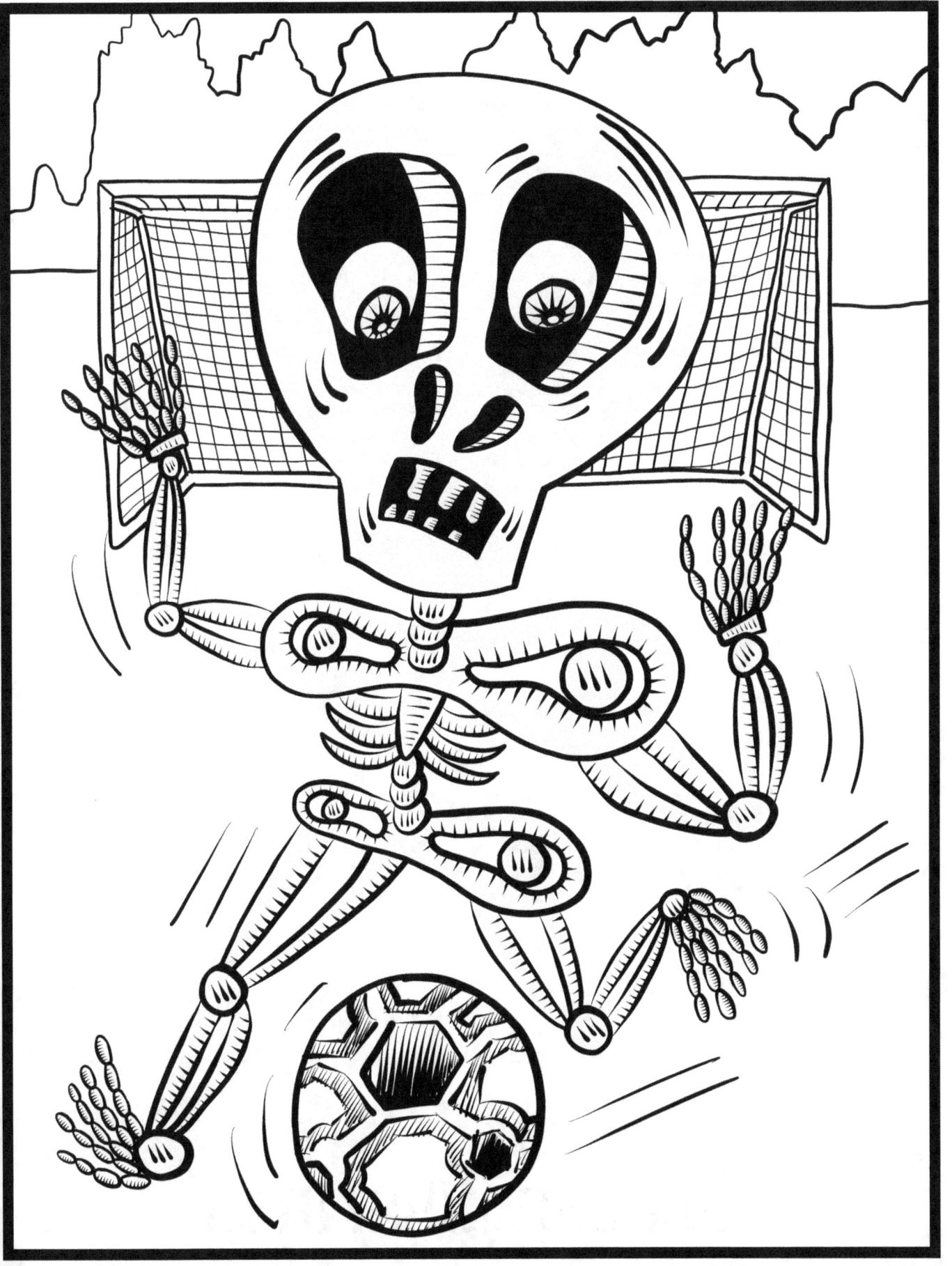

Soccer Sherman

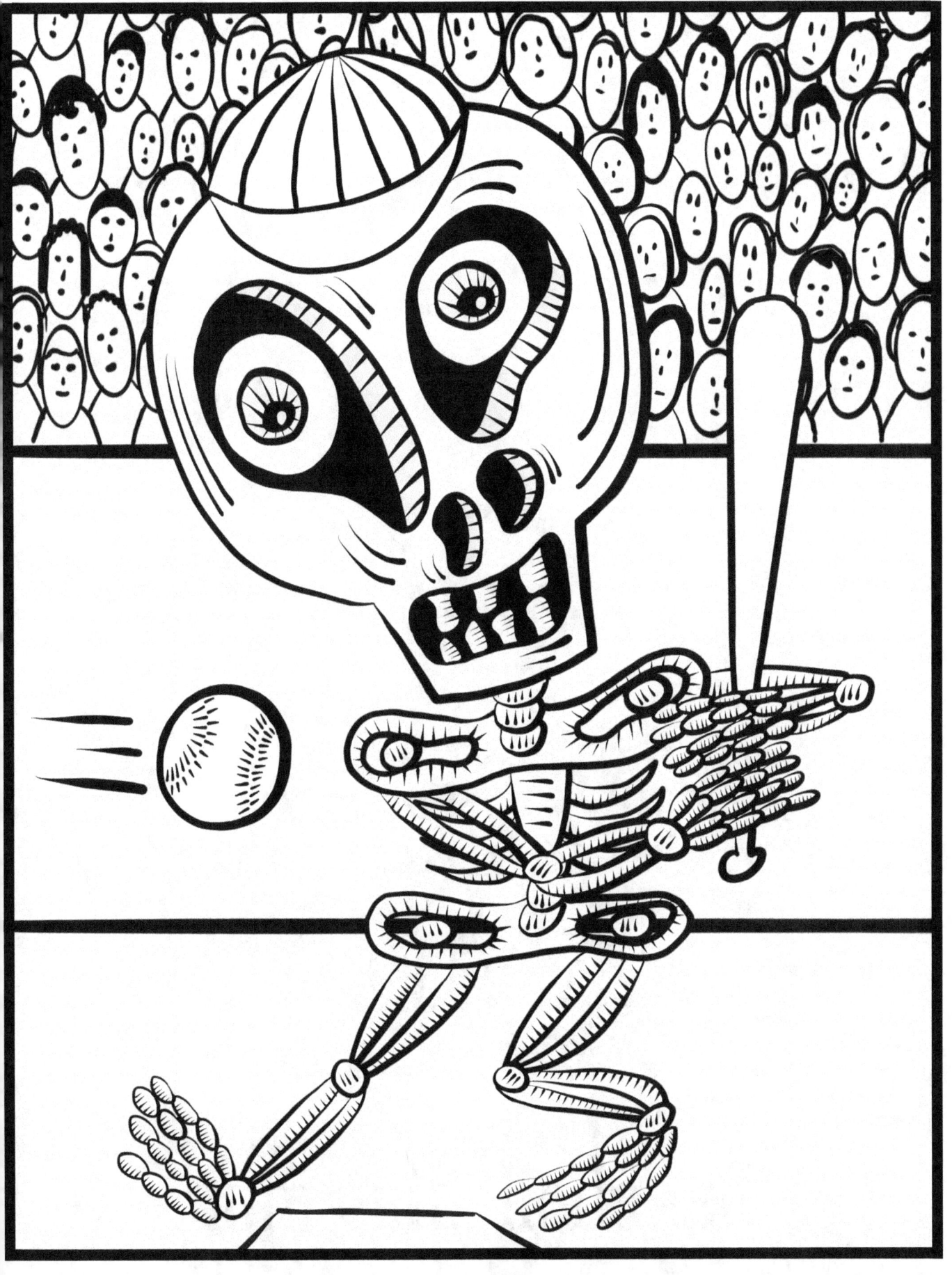

Baseball Sherman

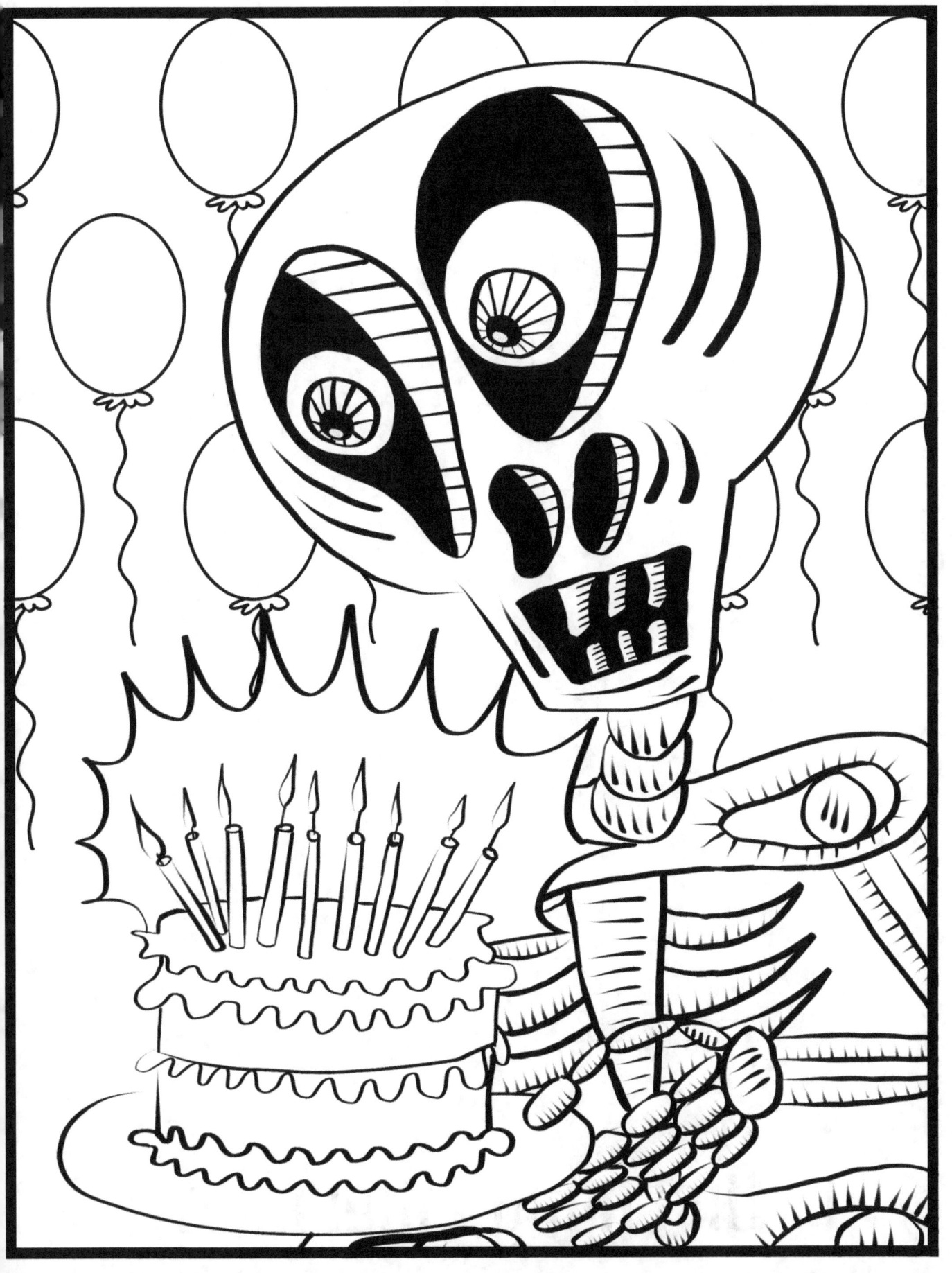

Birthday Sherman

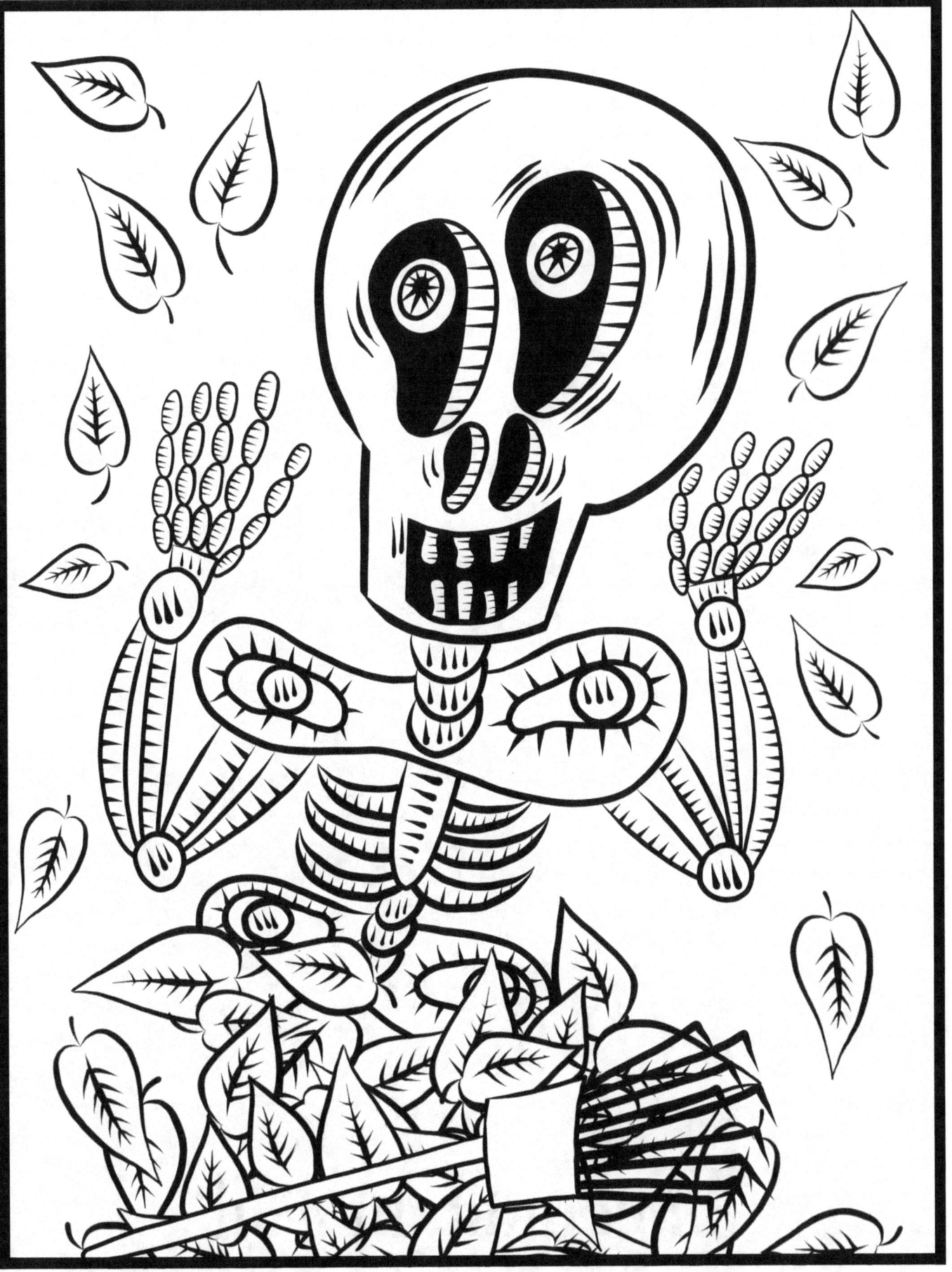

Sherman in Fall

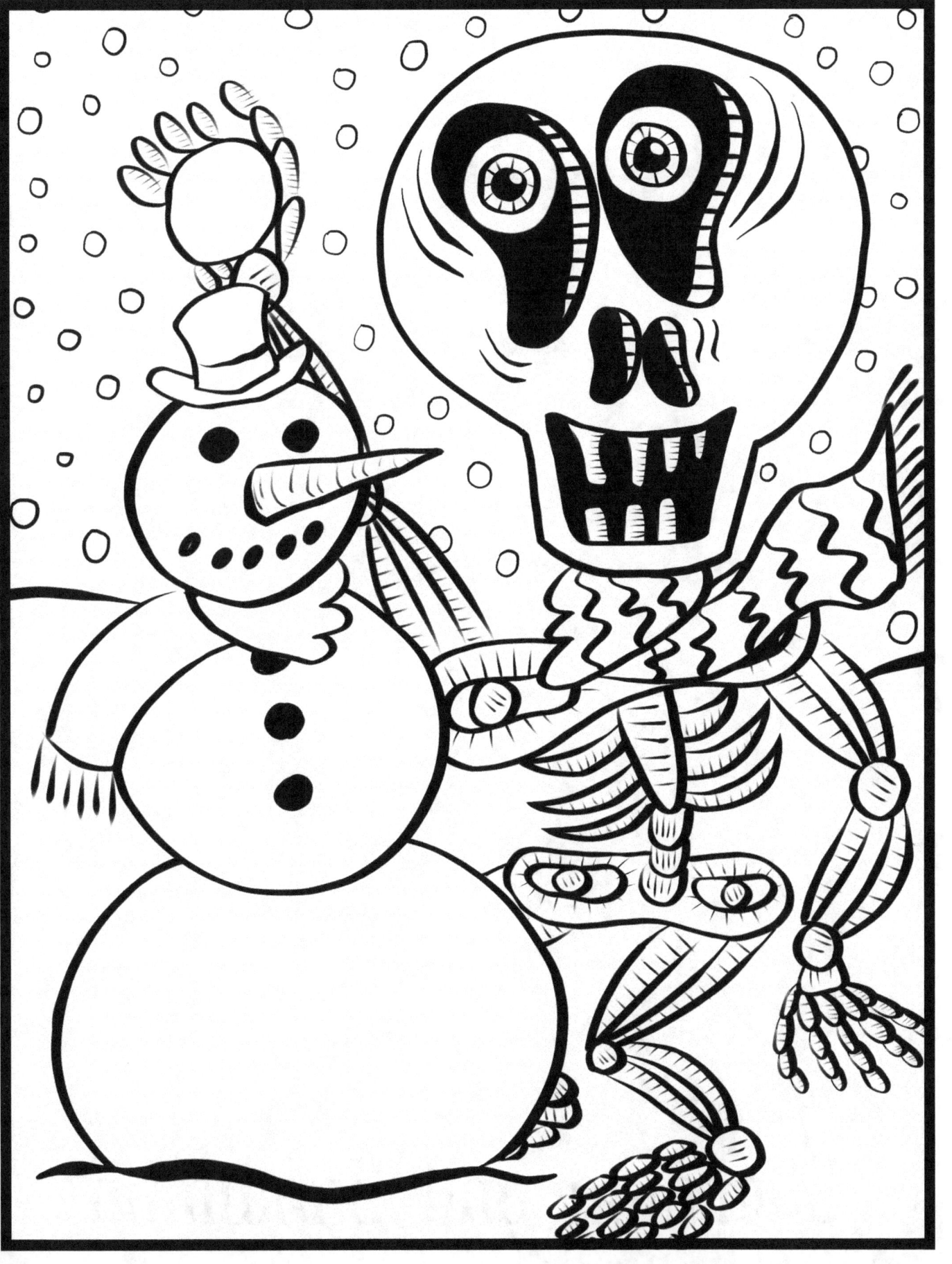

Sherman and Snowman

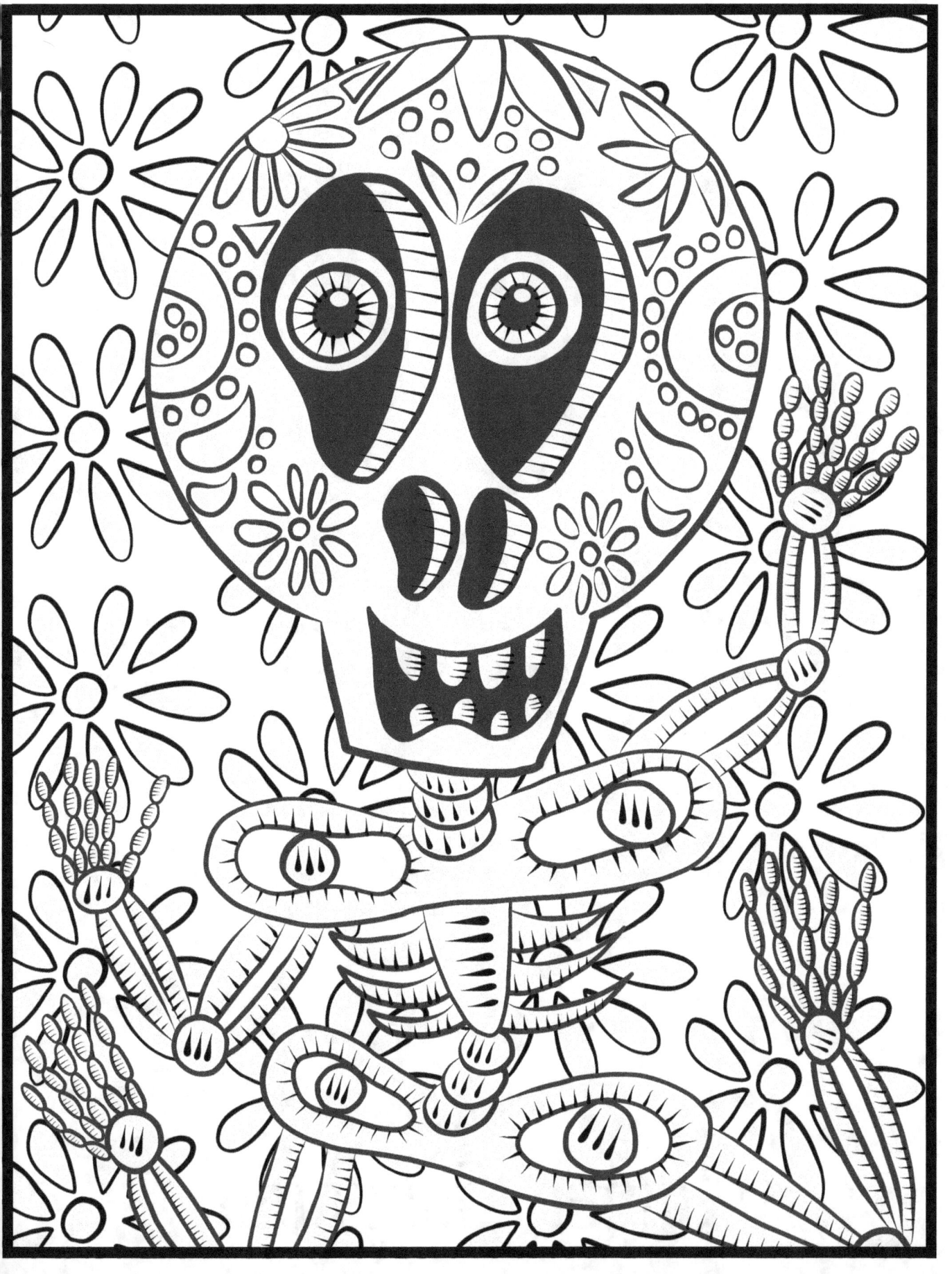

Sugar Sherman

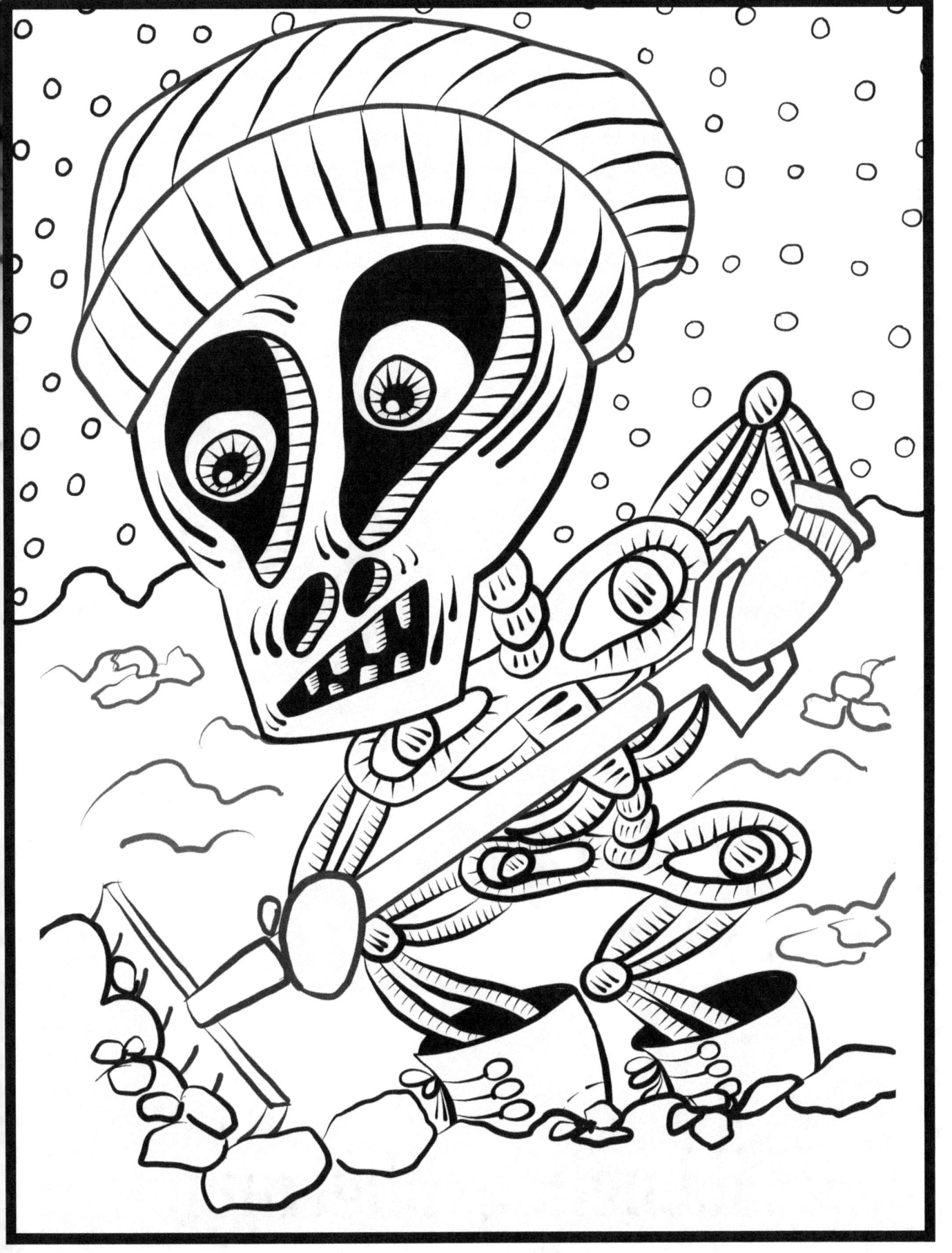

Shoveling Sherman

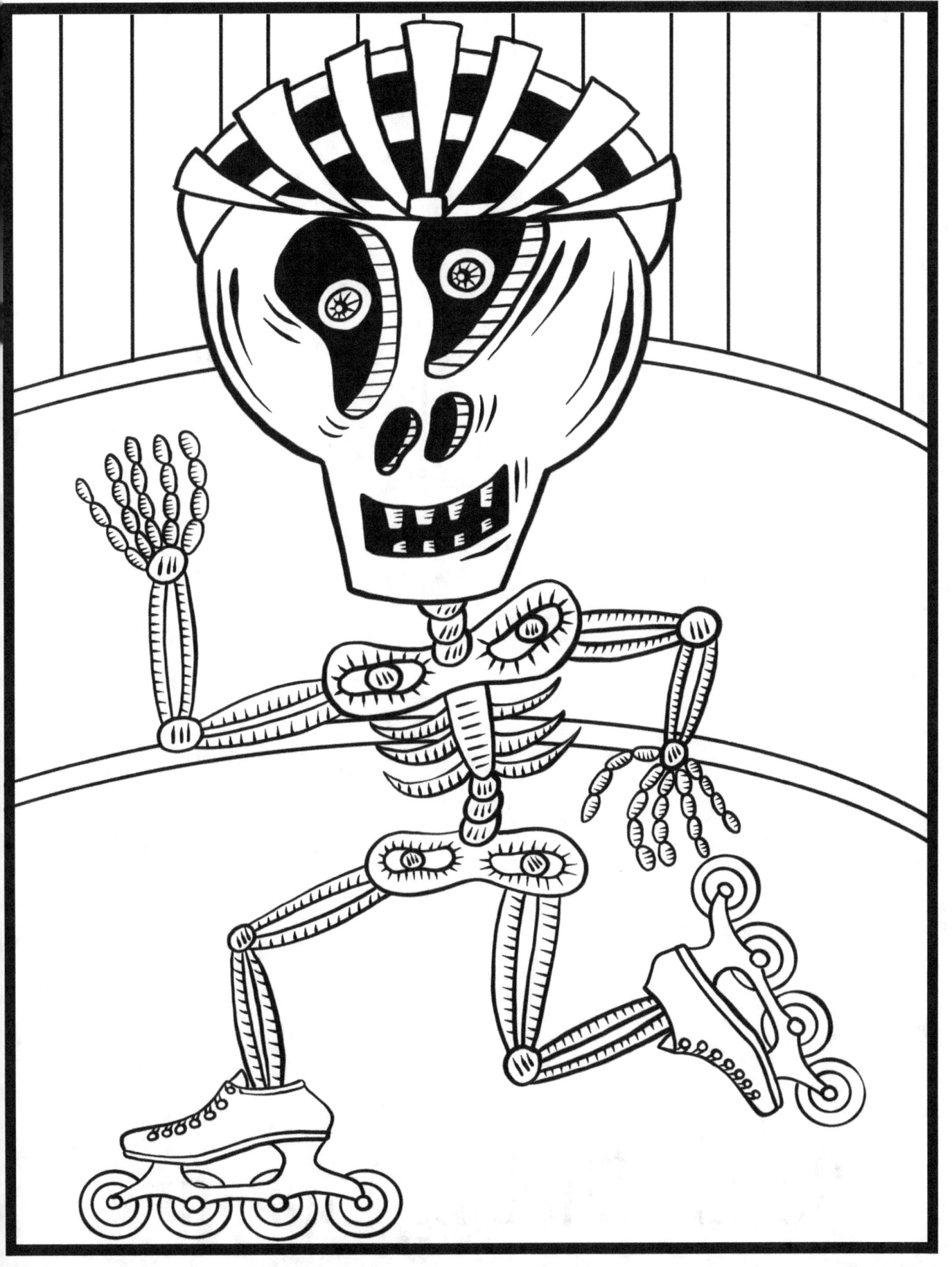

Roller Skating Sherman